Living Under Glass

ABOVE: *The Conservatory at Harlaxton Manor, Lincolnshire, England.*

JANE TRESIDDER & STAFFORD CLIFF

Living Under Glass

Clarkson N. Potter, Inc./Publishers
DISTRIBUTED BY CROWN PUBLISHERS, INC., NEW YORK

For Jack Tresidder
and Susan Collier

Publisher's Note: This book contains guidelines and instructions for home construction projects, which the reader is advised to read and follow with care. Consult an expert if adapting designs from the book.

Copyright © 1986 by Jane Tresidder and Stafford Cliff

CLARKSON N. POTTER, POTTER, and colophon are trademarks of Clarkson N. Potter, Inc.

Published by Clarkson N. Potter, Inc., 225 Park Avenue South, New York, New York 10003, and represented in Canada by the Canadian MANDA Group

Library of Congress Cataloging-in-Publication Data
Tresidder, Jane.
Living under glass.

Includes index
1. Conservatories.   2. Garden rooms.   3. Interior decoration.   4. Glass construction.   I. Cliff, Stafford. II. Title
NA8360.T74   1986   728'.9
85-19152
ISBN 0-517-55610-3
10 9 8 7 6 5 4 3 2 1
First Edition

RIGHT: Before it was renovated, this Victorian conservatory, attached to eighteenth-century Maperton House, in Somerset, England, was little more than stone walls topped with a tangle of rusting ironwork. Now beautifully restored as a summer sitting room, the extension encloses a pond where weed-eating carp browse.

CONTENTS

INTRODUCTION

The rise of the domestic conservatory in nineteenth-century England was one of the most enchanting by-products of the Industrial Revolution. By a happy coincidence of timing, the technology of glass and iron construction developed in step with an increased interest in exotic plants, making it possible for even middle-class people to display their botanical acquisitions in glass structures attached to their houses; the idea of plants and people living together under glass followed. The idea was essentially a romantic one, a response to the worship of nature which emerged in eighteenth-century France and was subsequently taken up by the wealthy classes throughout Europe, often with passionate enthusiasm. Of course, domestic conservatories appeared in many other countries, but it was England that led the fashion and English architecture that was responsible for the most original innovations in conservatory construction. The historical sections of this book reflect this dominance, and their illustrations are in large part a celebration of the Victorian conservatory—ranging from the grandest freestanding structures of ballroom size to the more modest charms of glassed-in spaces that are hardly more than extensions to suburban drawing rooms.

ABOVE: A formal Victorian tea party takes place on a tranquil afternoon.

From the beginning, conservatories seem to have freed the imagination of architects and designers in a unique way. Conservatories were designed to let in light, to show off plants and flowers to dramatic effect, to impress and to entertain—purposes that had little in common with the more functional demands of other areas of the house. Above all, they spoke of pleasure and leisure. They were characteristically graceful and ornamental, with a purity enforced by the limited range of materials that could be used in their construction—essentially glass with a ribbing of iron or wood.

These qualities remain features of conservatories today and are the consistent link between two very different design approaches.

On the one hand are conservatories consciously based on Victorian traditions, with arches, curvilinear forms, and extravagant decorative embellishments. The impetus for this approach has come, naturally, from England itself, where conservatories went out of fashion for half a century and began to reappear only in the 1960s, when postwar austerity was left behind and it became possible again to think of the pleasures of making living space for plants.

Nostalgia has been a significant element in this revival. Few parts of a house can better complement Victorian-style furniture, ornaments, pictures, and fabrics than a conservatory with basket chairs, ceramic jardinieres, and palms. Today there are flourishing businesses producing reproductions of Victorian conservatories, often in modular form, which can be added to a wide range of buildings, from small townhouses to country mansions.

The other design approach owes more to America and Europe, especially Germany. It draws on the achievements of modern architecture in glass to create structures that range from simple glazed extensions to dramatic buildings—even complete houses in glass—that in excitement, novelty, and spectacle rival anything the Victorians produced.

The conservatory of today is usually more a living space for people than simply a showplace for plants. Modern technology has made possible a balance of temperature and ventilation that allows a multiplicity of functions. What remains constant, as the hundreds of photographs in this book show, is the distinctive magic and beauty of spaces filled with light and living things.

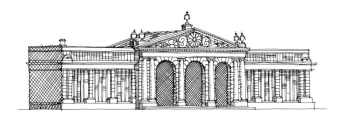

THE HISTORY OF THE CONSERVATORY

The modern technology of building with glass is relatively recent, but the idea of sheltering plants from the cold is an ancient one. In the first century A.D., the Romans, who had acquired a taste for many of the exotic vegetables and fruits grown in the warmer countries of their empire, learned to cultivate gherkins and melons in trays that on cold nights could be wheeled into the shelter of nearby caves. More sophisticated techniques were also developed. The celebrated naturalist Pliny tells us that the emperor Tiberius enjoyed cucumbers grown in forcing stoves in his gardens, and refers to *lapis specularis*, transparent stone such as selenite or mica, which was used in thin sheets to cover beds sunk in pits heated by fermenting manure or by burning dry manure or wood. During the Middle Ages Roman technology was largely forgotten in Europe, and plants were left to survive as best they could, apart from the shelter provided by walls and surrounding buildings, such as cloisters. It was not until the sixteenth century, when the first botanical gardens were established, that the protection of plants began to be studied and special buildings constructed. The earliest of these experimental gardens was founded in Pisa in 1543, and the idea soon spread to other parts of Italy and Europe.

Delicate fruit trees such as sour oranges were grown inside shelters that were designed to regulate light and air.

LEFT: An early-eighteenth-century "wintering gallery" in Holland's Leyden University Botanic Gardens.

Modest enclosures of wood or masonry, known as wintering sheds, were equipped with small fires, charcoal braziers, and sometimes wax candles to keep the plants warm. The first description of a greenhouse, known as a "stove," used for heating plants was in the agriculturalist Oliver de Sèvres's account of a remarkable wooden shed built in the late sixteenth century at Heidelberg for the Elector of Pfalz. The shed was ventilated by large shutters which could be readily opened and closed. By the seventeenth century the simple shuttered enclosures that had been used to protect sour orange trees had begun to be replaced by orangeries, completely enclosed structures built of wood, brick, or stone, usually with vertical leaded windows in the south walls. These were first used in the Netherlands, and were very simple in design. Later, as the fashion for such structures spread to other countries, the designs became more complex. The French introduced windows with rounded arches, and the Germans produced baroque forms on an increasingly grand scale.

Generally there were windows in the south walls, and heat was provided by iron furnaces burning peat or tile ones stoked with wood. More sophisticated models produced heat by convection rather than radiation, making it less likely that delicate leaves would be scorched. After the Restoration in Britain in 1660, orangeries came to be called greenhouses or conservatories, owing perhaps to the increasingly wide range of plants grown in their shelter. Lemons and myrtles and other "exotic greens" joined the orange trees. During the eighteenth and early nineteenth centuries, grapevines and cultivation of the pineapple became fashionable, acquiring such importance that separate greenhouses were specially devoted to them. In a sense, this was a continuation of the original Roman emphasis on growing edible rather than merely decorative plants. However, toward the end of the seventeenth century came a new development that was to lead to one of the most important uses of the conservatory in its nineteenth-century heyday: orangeries began to be used not just for the cultivation of delicate plants but as rooms for entertainment.

As T. Langford, an English writer of the late seventeenth century, recorded: "Greenhouses are of late built as ornaments to Gardens . . . as well as for Conservatories for tender plants; and when the Curiosities in the Summer time are dispersed in their proper places in the Garden, the House being accommodated for that purpose may serve for an entertaining room."

One such place in England was the Hampton Court orangery built for Queen Anne by Sir Christopher Wren and Sir John Vanbrugh in 1704. Novelist Daniel Defoe wrote that the queen "often was pleased to make the Green House, which is very beautiful, her summer Supper House."

The Dutch and the English were pioneering methods of heating as well. Bark- and manure-burning stoves were built under floors, with smoke flues leading off them into the greenhouses in various ingenious ways. The English diarist and gardening enthusiast John Evelyn, impressed by the ingenuity of the nurseryman at the Chelsea Physic Garden, referred to "subterraneous heat conveyed by a stove under the conservatory, all vaulted with brick, so he has the doors and windows open in the hardest frosts, secluding only the snow."

Early in the eighteenth century the Dutch scientist Dr. Hermann Boerhaave developed the idea of using sloping glass to obtain more light in orangeries, and by the 1730s various types of experimental lean-to greenhouses had been constructed in Holland's Leyden Botanical Gardens, some with glass roofs, others with glass in the side walls as well.

Architecturally, the nineteenth century was the golden age of conservatory building. Britain's industrial advances together with the English love of gardening produced an interest in exotic plants under glass not only in grand society but also among middle-class families throughout the country. The social climate was changing as wealth flowing from the Industrial Revolution was increasingly widely distributed. The newly affluent built villas on small plots of land and attached conservatories to them as symbols of their newly achieved status in the contemporary social order.

Technical improvements in glass manufacture and iron construction helped expand architectural possibilities. First, new glassmaking methods were discovered whereby glass could be produced in sheets of up to six feet in length, about three times the size previously possible. Second, more flexible, less unwieldy framing was developed from cast iron, leading to the construction of ever more elegant vaults and domes.

Changes in heat technology led to the replacement of primitive stoves by boilers which could be placed outside the greenhouses, providing heat by the circulation of hot water in pipes running through the building. By improving the distribution and control of heat and by avoiding the production of fumes in the greenhouse, yet more exotic plants could be grown.

Better heating in conjunction with new combinations of materials which helped give the necessary light made it possible to cultivate tropical and subtropical trees and palms, and the marriage of clarity with strength led architects to produce charming and whimsical, increasingly extravagant glass follies.

ABOVE RIGHT: Pergolas were the predecessors of orangeries and conservatories. In this early-seventeenth-century German engraving by Paul Furst, fashionable diners are protected from the sun by a curved, though unglazed, pergola.

RIGHT: A late-seventeenth-century engraving of the Duc d'Arenberg's park, near Brussels, shows a summer view of the orangery with potted citrus trees arranged outside.

Nature, safely domesticated in a conservatory, could provide a complete contrast to the formality of the drawing room—a living area that could emulate a simple summer garden, establish a haven of classical fountains and statuary, or even dramatically suggest a fantasy jungle.

Any conservatory maintains a delicate balance between heat and ventilation, light and shade. Too much heat and plants steam to death in their own condensation; too much ventilation and it becomes impossible to raise the temperature to the appropriate level; too much light and plants scorch and die of overheating in summer; too much shade and they become yellow and spindly.

It requires considerable ingenuity to achieve the right balance. Many problems during the eighteenth century resulted from the character of the glass, which was characteristically of the rippled and blemished "broad and crown" type. In England, where many of the important technical advances were achieved, glass was taxed according to its weight, but sold to the customer at a price related to its dimensions. Naturally, manufacturers tended to produce the thinnest glass possible, and as a result it could be used practically only in inconveniently small panes. In conservatory glazing, the small overlapping panes and the size of the bars needed for strength to support the glass made early interiors rather gloomy. Flaws in the glass and the overlaps themselves blocked out light and caused further problems. Dirt was trapped, water seeping between the panes by capillary action encouraged the growth of minute mosslike plants, and in the winter freezing water shattered the glass.

ABOVE LEFT AND LEFT: The Crystal Palace was the first large-scale prefabricated building of its kind and symbolized the Victorian's advances in combining technological brilliance with creative splendor. Both of these photographs were taken after the Great Exhibition of 1851 when the building had been re-sited in Sydenham, South London.

RIGHT: A favorite Sunday outing for Victorian Londoners was a visit to the Palm House at Kew.

In the nineteenth century technical developments began to provide solutions to the problems encountered by the early designers of conservatories. In 1833 the introduction into Britain of good-quality cylinder-manufactured glass was a major advance (the French having developed a form of sheet glass in Lorraine some years previously). With the abolition of the glass tax in Britain in 1845, large panes could be used without financial penalty.

However, these advances brought new problems. The larger panes seemed to encourage scorching of the plants beneath.

The first remedy proposed was tinted glass, first introduced at the great Palm House in Kew (see page 11). In fact the experiment was a failure, as the plants did better later when the yellow-green tinted glass was changed back to clear panes.

The early experiments with tinted glass did at least have the useful result of eliminating manganese oxide in glass manufacture. With exposure to sunlight this chemical gradually discolored the glass, causing it to turn a pinkish color which actually intensified the scorching.

Another cause of botanical sunburn was the uneven surface of the sheet glass being produced at the end of the nineteenth century. Cockles or variations in thickness produced during the manufacturing process formed spots which, like lenses, focused damaging beams of light with almost laserlike intensity on the delicate plants. This drawback eventually led to the production of a type of rolled plate glass whose irregular ribbed surface not only prevented any harmful concentrations of light but also reduced the need to shade plants in hot weather.

Until the Industrial Revolution began in the late eighteenth century, all iron was wrought. It never became completely molten beyond a paste stage at which it could be hammered into shape. From 1780 onward, cast iron began to be produced, molded from its molten state. It was weaker than wrought iron and more liable to fracture under lateral stress. Thus, in the nineteenth century each type of iron tended to be used for its special qualities. Cast iron was used in large supporting columns and for smaller load-bearing components like baseplates and brackets, while wrought iron began to compete for favor with wood as a more flexible material for beams and glazing bars.

The Great Exhibition Building (Crystal Palace) built in 1851 was hailed as a pioneering example of the combination of iron and glass, but in fact less iron was used than is generally supposed. The columns and the main girders were iron, but the roof and upper floors and the arches over the transepts were of wood, as was the external cladding, apart from some decorative iron details. Nevertheless, there is no doubt that this remarkable building contributed to the general acceptance of the idea of ironwork framing.

The design of the Crystal Palace was the result of a royal commission to produce the "largest building that the world has ever seen."

As Charles Dickens wrote in his newspaper column "Household Words": "Two parties in London, relying on the accuracy and good faith of certain iron-masters, glass-workers in the provinces and of one master-carpenter in London, bound themselves for a certain sum and in the course of four months to cover 18 acres of ground, with a building upwards of a third of a mile long."

The "certain sum" was £79,000—about $100,000—and the two parties were the engineer Charles Fox, of Fox and Henderson, and Robert Lucas Chance, a Birmingham glass manufacturer. The master carpenter was a Mr. Birch of the Phoenix Sawmills, and the brilliant and original design was produced in less than three weeks by Sir Joseph Paxton. One of the building's most beautiful features, the arched transept, was in fact born of necessity after public outcry against the proposed felling of a row of elms that ran across the center of the site.

The Horticultural (later the Royal Horticultural) Society members were always fascinated by scientific advances in anything to do with botanical exotica. The conservatory shown at upper right was commissioned from John Claudius Loudon by the society's Joseph Sabine. Loudon probably intended to glaze it with shallow "ridge and furrow"—long bands of peaked glass roofing—to catch the "two daily meridians" of the sun. Other elements typical of Loudon's designs include the solid back wall, which helped to retain warmth and the underground heating.

Architect George Tod was a hothouse enthusiast who was particularly interested in aquatic houses. This enthusiasm derived from the discovery, by Sir Robert Schomburgk in British Guiana in 1837, of the giant South American water lily. Although seeds had previously been planted at Kew in 1846, Paxton was the first to produce actual flowers in his heated stove at Chatsworth. Triumphantly he presented a rare bloom to Queen Victoria later that year, and the huge plant was renamed Victoria Regia in her honor. Nervous Victorian children were made to stand on a leaf to demonstrate to their fascinated parents its remarkable size and strength.

RIGHT: Another imaginative design by John Claudius Loudon, this hothouse was commissioned in 1818 by Joseph Sabine of the Horticultural Society. Loudon probably intended to glaze it with shallow "ridge and furrow"—long bands of peaked glass roofing—to catch the "two daily meridians" of the sun. Other typical elements of Loudon's designs include the solid back wall to retain warmth and the underground heating system.

RIGHT: Conservatory design has changed remarkably little since this cutaway sketch appeared in Messenger and Company's late nineteenth-century catalog.

The Great Innovators

Nathaniel Bagshaw Ward
1791–1868

The son of a doctor, Nathaniel Ward spent his childhood collecting plants and insects, and it was his boyhood interest in plants that led to his avocation. Although he followed his father into medical practice, he still found time to carry out botanical research and experimentation. He was particularly fascinated by ferns, which he tried to cultivate in his garden at Finsbury Circus, but with little success because of the high levels of air pollution in London. In the summer of 1829 he made an experiment with mold enclosed in a wide-mouthed glass-lidded jar. He noticed that the moisture generated by the mold would rise up the jar, condense on the glass, then return to the mold. This kept the moisture level in the jar always the same. After about a week he discovered that grass and fern seedlings were beginning to grow out of the mold. Here was the answer to his problem—a container which would protect exotic plants from a hostile environment and at the same time provide the heat, moisture, and air necessary for their growth. Ward, however, was not the first to discover this phenomenon. A Scotsman, Alan Maconochie, had in 1825 already invented a miniature wooden greenhouse with a glass top. When Ward announced his success, Maconochie was modest enough not to claim credit. In 1833 Ward put his experiment to the test. Having planted ferns and grasses in two specially built glass cases, he shipped them to Syd-

ney, Australia, then a voyage of several months. The plants arrived safely and the following year were sent back to England. During all this time they were never watered, yet they showed no signs of deterioration when they reached their destination.

The Wardian case, as this mini-greenhouse came to be known, satisfied collectors' needs for a safe way to transport exotic plants. By the 1840s Ward's invention had become a fashionable way of displaying exotic plants and ferns, and wealthy collectors employed wood-carvers, gilders, and enamelers to create fantastical designs for the cases.

John Claudius Loudon
1783–1843

Loudon's life was a model of hard work and determination, and his influence on horticulture reflects his enormous creative energy.

Born into a Scottish farming family, he was deeply interested in gardening even as a child. After attending school in Edinburgh, he worked as an apprentice to a nurseryman and landscape gardener. Not content to consider this full-time employment, he furthered his studies in other subjects, such as linguistics.

One of Loudon's particular interests was the development of greenhouses. He dreamed of "winding walks, fountains and even plots of grasses and ponds of water, so that the only difference between them and real gardens is, that glass intervenes between the summit of their trees and the sky. . . ."

In 1816 he began turning his dreams into reality by designing a

domed glass structure based on slender wrought iron sash bars holding small overlapping panes. Realizing the commercial potential of his innovation, Loudon teamed up with the building firm W. & D. Bailey to construct greenhouses for the public.

So that potential customers could see completed examples of his work, Loudon built prototypes in the garden of his home at Porchester Terrace in Bayswater, London. In his demonstration model he incorporated thirteen bars and seven different shapes of glass, with some sections of corrugated iron and specially treated paper, to show the versatility of its design. Loudon had achieved his aim: "to make English hot-houses look beautiful in their own right instead of being merely lean-to glazed sheds."

Unfortunately, Loudon gained little financial benefit from his association with the Baileys. In 1818, in order to give more time to his other interests, he conceded his design rights to them. Because of this, his outstanding contribution to the development of the Victorian conservatory is sometimes overlooked by historians.

Decimus Burton
1800–81

Of all the professional nineteenth-century architects, Burton was the most interested in the technicalities of glass and iron construction.

He was the tenth son of James Burton, a successful speculative builder who designed many streets and squares in the north part of London's Bloomsbury. Having trained in his father's office, Burton set up his own practice in 1821 and specialized in extensive town planning schemes.

Apart from the famous Palm House at Kew, in Surrey, Burton's most spectacular conservatory was the Winter Garden (1846) in Regent's Park, London, on which he collaborated with Richard Turner, the Dublin engineer (see Turner). Commissioned by the Royal Botanic Society, the conservatory really was a garden, with an earthen floor topped first with gravel and then with a layer of gleaming white powdered shell. Very light and elegant, the building covered an area of nineteen thousand square feet and was, for that time, unusually informal. Plants grew in "natural" clumps, and pots of fragrant flowers and prized specimen plants stood on numerous small iron tables. The curved-ridge roofs seemed to float on the hollow cast iron columns, through which rainwater ran into underground cisterns. Decorative panels of red and blue glass added glancing patterns of light to make an enchanting setting for the flower shows and fetes that were regularly held there.

Sir Joseph Paxton
1803–65

The seventh son of a Bedfordshire farmer, Joseph Paxton was born at Milton Bryan, near Woburn, Bedfordshire. He began his working life as an apprentice gardener and later went on to work at the newly opened gardens of the Horticultural Society, which were leased from the sixth Duke of Devonshire. Impressed with Paxton's ideas, in 1826 the duke appointed him head gardener at Chatsworth, the duke's splendid Derbyshire estate. Paxton was to prove a worthy choice. He threw himself into his duties with great energy and set about restoring the formal gardens. Gradually the duke, realizing Paxton's worth, encouraged the latter to assist him with his business interests and to accompany him on trips abroad. Paxton's travels helped nurture his interest in exotic plants. He became a great botanical collector, often commissioning plant hunters to search for rare examples. His reputation as a botanist and propagator was enhanced by his architectural skills. He designed a series of increasingly ingenious glass, wood, and iron buildings, of which the most famous example was his Great Conservatory at Chatsworth, Derbyshire, a tropical landscape under glass. This led directly to Paxton's patent system of construction in glass, and subsequently to the magnificent design for the Crystal Palace.

Although himself a great technical innovator, Paxton often adopted architectural and gardening styles developed by others, especially Loudon. One of Paxton's major architectural contributions was his recognition of the virtue of using prefabricated parts, which could be adapted for buildings of any dimension (see Crystal Palace, page 11).

Paxton was the epitome of the new self-made Victorian man; through his own ingenuity he became a financier, landscape gardener, town planner, architect, and politician. His work with glass buildings, particularly with the Crystal Palace, gave tremendous impetus to the construction of conservatories.

Richard Turner
1798–1881

Turner was an iron founder, with highly original ideas. In 1836 he began working from the Hammersmith Iron Works, Shelburne Road, Dublin, a foundry that became linked with many of the great greenhouses of the period.

One of his company's first commissions was the construction of the two wings of the Palm House in Belfast. This building, designed by Charles Lanyon, was started in June 1839, before Kew or Glasnevin, Dublin, but was not completed until 1886. By that time it measured 362 feet in length, with a width of 100 feet at the center, above which the summit of the lantern reached 66 feet.

With Decimus Burton, Turner worked on the Palm House at Kew, where he was concerned with the detailing, prefabrication, and engineering (see Palm House, Kew, page 11). He would have been gratified by the following description of it: "One of the very finest plant houses in the world. Its graceful lines and admirable proportions made it as pleasing to the eye as it is possible for a structure of glass and iron to be."

Another of his major projects, again in partnership with Burton, was the Winter Garden at Regent's Park (see Decimus Burton, page 8). It has been said that Burton originally wanted it to be framed partly in wood and that it was Turner who suggested the exclusive use of glass and iron. In Ireland he was kept busy with work on the Conservatory at Killikee in County Dublin, the vinery at the Vice-Regal Lodge in Phoenix Park, Dublin, and the central dome and second wing of the Curvilinear Range, at the National Botanic Gardens, Glasnevin, which was completed in 1850.

Also in this year, together with his architect brother Thomas, he submitted a design for the Great Exhibition Building. This was an adventurous scheme for a building nearly 2,000 feet long and over 4,000 feet wide based partly on his recently completed design for the Lime Street Station roof at Liverpool. It would have been a whimsical blend of railway station and cathedral crowned with a palm house. It was, however, found to be too expensive to build, so London missed out on a truly extraordinary landmark.

Rare Pavilions

The Conservatory
Syon House, Middlesex, 1820–27

The Palm House
Bicton Gardens, Devon, c. 1818–38

The Great Conservatory
Chatsworth, Derbyshire, 1836–40

In the early part of the nineteenth century the Duke of Northumberland employed a young architect, Charles Fowler (1791–1867), to design a conservatory for him at Syon, his estate opposite Kew.

A keen botanist, the duke wanted to display his exotic treasures in a building worthy of them and in which they would flourish. The result was a magnificent 280-foot-long glass structure with a massive Italianate dome at its center, flanked by two long curved aisles, each ending at a glass pavilion. Fowler's architectural style incorporated various elements from both the baroque orangery and the nineteenth-century conservatory. He tried to reconcile his two principal goals: to bring the maximum amount of light into the building and to adhere to traditional architectural forms normally built in stone. Loudon's influence can be seen in Fowler's inclusion of the large central glass dome. This dome, however, is unusual in that it sits upon four saddleback roofs of a rectangular building and is supported by an inner arcade of cast iron columns. The cast iron pillars and trusses throughout the building were specially made, but the wrought iron bars were of standard manufacture.

The semicircular shape of the building protected the garden, making it a pleasant place to wander in all seasons.

An interesting early example of glass house construction is the Palm House at Bicton Gardens near East Budleigh in Devon. There are no records of who designed or built it or even when it was built. However, given the style of the building and its inclusion in a map dated 1838, it is possible that W. & D. Bailey were the builders and that it was based on Loudon's design.

It is a curvilinear building, 68 feet long and 33 feet at its widest point. The central section is rectangular, flanked by two domed quadrants, with a domed semicircle.

Technically, it is a lean-to greenhouse, built against, but slightly below, a north-facing stone wall, so that it would follow the profile of the wall. The whole structure contains only two internal cast iron columns, overall support being provided by wrought iron sash bars. Toward the apex of the roof domes, these bars decrease in number, two merging into one, so that the width of the glass panes remains the same.

The use of small, straight glass panes made it possible to glaze the curved surface quite easily (larger panes would have had to be curved). This method of glazing produces a fish-scale effect.

Ventilation is controlled by flaps in the wall against which the building stands and in the ridge of the roof, where they can be swiveled to provide free airflow.

One of the most famous Victorian conservatories, this building was 277 feet long, 123 feet wide, and 67 feet high. The biggest privately owned glass structure then in existence, it housed the Duke of Devonshire's collection of exotic trees and plants. Although Joseph Paxton designed it, Decimus Burton was brought in as a consultant, and there was, and still is, much controversy over the exact contribution that each made.

Paxton's design incorporated a wooden framework for the curvilinear structure with a ridge-and-furrow roof. Cast iron was used only for the pillars and the internal gallery, the sash bars being made of wood.

One of Paxton's principles of garden architecture was that a conservatory should be at a discreet distance from the house: "But there is one edifice totally opposite to a residence which requires more complete and decided isolation, and must be situated in a spot where its own influence can be felt. This is the Conservatory which should not be near the Mansion." So the Great Conservatory was built on a leveled clearing in a wood in the park.

It housed the first and most representative collection of tropical plants in England, "a building and collection of plants so grand and rare as to be deservedly ranked among the minor wonders of England." Palms and banana trees grew quite naturally amid the delicate ferns and minute aquatic plants.

The Palm House
Kew, Surrey, 1844–48

One of the most inspiring and imposing greenhouses in the world, the Palm House is the centerpiece of the Royal Gardens at Kew, founded by Prince Frederick, father of George III. This cast and wrought iron structure, which rests on a 3-foot-high stone plinth, is 362 feet long, with a transept 100 feet wide and 66 feet high and wings 50 feet wide. It was built by Richard Turner's Hammersmith Foundry, but responsibility for the actual design is rather harder to establish. For a long time Turner and Decimus Burton submitted alternative rival schemes, each publicly and savagely criticizing the other's proposals. Eventually Turner, apparently acquiescent, submitted his bid for building one of Burton's designs. Once he was given the commission, he then changed the design, making a revolutionary wrought iron structure which was a quarter of the weight of Burton's (and therefore let in much more light). While his tactics were a little Machiavellian, Turner's technology was brilliant and the result was outstanding. The architect had begun to command his materials. The nearby watering tower is a remarkable and eccentric feature, a replica of a typical Italian campanile. Near its summit, almost 107 feet above the ground, is a reservoir which provides sufficient pressure to water the tallest palms from above. The central building, 65 feet high, houses the tallest palms and has a viewing gallery reached from two spiral staircases.

The Crystal Palace
London, 1850–51

By the middle of the nineteenth century, Victorian industry and commerce were booming. The newly prosperous middle class was delighted when Albert, the Prince Consort, decided it was time to show the flag to the rest of the world. His plan, a happy combination of a demonstration of British commercial and industrial superiority with a statement of universal peace and brotherhood, culminated in the idea of presenting a Great Exhibition under one roof.

For this momentous undertaking, a Royal Commission was set up and a Building Committee formed to receive and evaluate designs and tenders. By the closing date for submissions no suitable applicant had been found, and the Building Committee decided to draw up a design of its own. It was considered so dreadful that Joseph Paxton was persuaded to submit a late entry. After much wrangling (one of his competitors was the redoubtable Richard Turner), Paxton's design was chosen, and on September 26, 1850, the first column of the Crystal Palace was put into position. The figures for the quantity of materials used are breathtaking: 900,000 square feet of glass, 372 roof trusses, 24 miles of guttering, 205 miles of sash bars, and 600,000 cubic feet of timber. After the transept and nave were marked out, the general arrangement consisted of a series of compartments 24 feet square by 24 feet high. Thackeray described the structure as "a rare pavilion, such as man saw, never since mankind began, and built and glazed!"

The New York Botanical Garden Conservatory
Bronx, New York, 1902

Directly inspired both by Britain's Palm House at Kew and the Crystal Palace, the conservatory in the New York Botanical Garden was designed by William R. Cobb and completed in 1902. Its outer walls were decorated in ornate Beaux Arts style, richer than the more restrained English taste, but much of this ornamentation as well as its classical entrance buildings were removed during two drastic modernizations in 1938 and 1953. Under its double-tiered central dome, 90 feet high and 100 feet wide, varieties of tropical and subtropical palms towered over walkways. Apart from the palm court, there were fourteen other connecting pavilions and galleries, each offering a different environment for various types of plants. Orchids mingled with ferns in a lush setting around a simulated volcanic crater, and at the other end of the humidity scale the American or New World desert house contained rare species of cacti. After the Second World War, this lovely building fell into disrepair, and some of its valuable plant specimens were irretrievably lost. Many years later the rekindling of public interest culminated in its being designated a city landmark by the New York Landmarks Preservation Commission in 1973. Through the generosity of a benefactor, Mrs. Enid A. Haupt, and under the direction of the architect Edward Larrabee Barnes, the building was sympathetically restored and reopened to the public in 1978 as the New York Botanical Garden's Enid A. Haupt Conservatory.

Fantasy Worlds

At the beginning of the nineteenth century, when the conservatory was a relatively recent innovation, most of the plants it contained were of temperate varieties. The idea was to bring them along with the attendant warmth and protection so that at a suitable maturity they could be taken out and planted in the garden.

Toward the middle of the century, however, it became fashionable to cultivate tropical flowering shrubs and climbers such as bright passionflowers, bougainvilleas, oddly flowered aristolochias, soft-scented jasmines, and colorful poincianas. Clerodendrons provided a patchwork made up of all the colors of the rainbow, the strange forms of orchids were exotic marvels, and the white flowers of angel's trumpet contributed a heady scent at night, which by day would fade and give way to the delicate fragrance of the white- and pink-flowered frangipani. Tropical climbers such as *Monstera deliciosa* were encouraged to twine around the great iron pillars.

LEFT: The great dome of Charles Fowler's Syon House conservatory rests on a pierced and arched (saddle) support on twelve cast iron columns finished to look like stone. Palms grow in a dense ground cover, while vines festoon the climbing frames.

RIGHT TOP: The nineteenth-century passion for ferns inspired much extravagant prose. Contemporary botanist Shirley Hibberd said that ferns kept a "coolness in the head and a freshness in the heart—breathings of a fragrance from the green world that sweeten the resting-places in the march of life."

RIGHT ABOVE: A smaller version of the limpid, nicknamed "dismal," pool which was a feature of the great conservatory that once stood at Chatsworth. Basket-weave brick now surrounds this delightful lily pond in today's more modest conservatory.

RIGHT: Casual abundance that changes with the season: these flowering shrubs are pot-grown, to be brought in at their peak and later banished once their glory is past.

Apart from a general effort to provide a myriad of colors, little thought was given at first to design. Plants were bedded in tubs and pots and grouped in a scientific and symmetrical way that appealed more to the botanist than to the aesthete. An exception to this rule was the tropical jungle under glass created and planted in "admirable disorder" by photographer/botanist John Dillwyn Llewellyn at Penllergaer, West Glamorgan, Wales, in 1843. Orchids were the dominant species here, displayed in an elaborate setting of mini-waterfalls, rapids, and pools amid a rambling profusion of ferns and lycopodia.

Interest in temperate plants reasserted itself in the second half of the nineteenth century and was confirmed by the construction of the Temperate House at Kew in the 1860s. At the same time, ferns became increasingly popular, so much so that some conservatories were wholly given over to these plants and became known as ferneries. A fine example can be seen at Château Impney, Hereford, where sculpture is set off by a rich display of ferns, carefully and artfully displayed for the greatest possible dramatic effect.

For easier cultivation, ferns were mostly planted in pots, which were skillfully hidden in rockeries. This trend away from formality brought about changes in the actual layout of conservatories. Rigidly straight aisles between the beds became winding lanes that followed the curves of the rockwork, producing a more casual and apparently haphazard effect. Thus, the fernery helped transform the conservatory from a botanical showcase into a miniature landscape, and new planting fashions further encouraged this.

The designs on these and the following two pages are by E. W. Godwin and Maurice B. Adams. They are taken from Artistic Conservatories, *a catalog published in 1880 by Messenger and Co., one of the best known conservatory builders in Loughborough, England.*

15

In the 1860s the French style of featuring subtropical plants with large, variegated, irregularly shaped leaves was imported into England. Lush, luxurious caladiums with massive heart-shaped leaves, brightly variegated dracaenas, brilliant-leaved crotons, and philodendrons were among the plants massed in beds in great profusion and skillfully arranged to create the illusion of a tropical jungle. Ferneries were also influenced by this influx, and tropical species were introduced, especially the splendid tree ferns.

The English writer Robert Kerr, in his book *The Gentleman's House*, published in 1875, gives an account of conservatories at this time: "The purpose in every such case is to accommodate, for gardening effect rather than mere conservation, a collection of rare plants to be kept in condition during winter by artificial heat, interspersed with sculptures, rock-work, shellwork, one or more fountains and so on, and the pillars shrouded in masses of creepers and pendant runners."

Edward William Godwin (1833–86) was one of the Victorian architects of the "Queen Anne revival," born of the Arts and Crafts movement with a dash of the sort of decorative Japanese-y touches pilloried in G. K. Chesterton's *The Man Who Was Thursday*. "Until now," Godwin said in 1880, "there has been little demand for artistic conservatories . . . however, we think we see that the tide is turning, and art seems about to be released from her prison within the four walls of the house and to assert her influence and charm over our gardens. It is a remarkable circumstance that our conservatories, the caskets in which we keep the highest works of art we possess—nature's art or flowers—should so long have remained so inartistic, so unworthy to set off their jewels.

"It is with a view to attempt to bear our part, in remedying this long-standing insult to our flowers that we issue these designs."

RIGHT: Photographs from the elegant catalog of Messenger and Co. show a plainer, more restrained style. All these were built onto country houses from the late 1890s to the early 1900s.

However, by the end of the 1880s there was another swing back to temperate plants. Rhododendrons, azaleas, and camellias became very popular, as did begonias, chrysanthemums, and other hardy herbaceous plants. The rockeries were taken over by primulas and various soft and pretty alpines.

Although some conservatories retained their abundant landscape interior, there was, especially in the Edwardian era, a movement toward change. Paths and aisles were dispensed with, and plants were put in pots and displayed on shelves along the walls. This allowed for more open space to accommodate garden furniture. Occasionally potted palms were grouped together as a small central feature and used as a backdrop for the furniture. Ease of maintenance and lowered heating costs led to the popularity of this style of conservatory and to its use primarily as an entertaining room with decorative plants —a function which survives today.

TOP, ABOVE, AND RIGHT: Here are more fantasy worlds in lovely old conservatories where ferns and other well-established planting produce a richly exotic effect.

Decline and Decay

Garden designer and writer William Robinson, in his book *English Flower Garden*, published in 1883, was the first to argue passionately for a return to nature, abandoning the expensive artificialities of the conservatory and cultivating the simple, the hardy, and the relatively inexpensive in the form of the old-fashioned cottage garden. Another strong influence on the growing public taste for a more relaxed style was that of a remarkable gardener, artist, and gentlewoman, Gertrude Jekyll. Toward the turn of the century, her ideas and Robinson's became increasingly popular among those in England who were beginning to see a need for social change, a breaking down of class barriers that were epitomized by rich living, formal gardens, and elaborate, "unnecessary" structures like conservatories. In fact, Robinson's views were so timely that his book eventually went into eight editions and six reprints. Some scholars have attributed the subsequent decline of the conservatory directly to criticisms in his books, such as these: "It is absurd to grow alternantheras in costly hothouses and not to give a place to flowers that endure cold as well as lilies of the valley." "For those who think of the beauty in our gardens and home landscapes, the placing of a glasshouse in the flower garden or pleasure garden is a serious matter, and some of the most interesting places in the country are defaced in this way." Robinson called for wild gardens, colorful, hardy herbaceous borders, rockeries, and a generally more informal approach to layout. Critic John Ruskin, who championed nature over industrialization, helped to deter en-

LEFT: A spectacular fire destroyed the main rooms of Gunton Park, Norfolk, in the 1880s during one of the Prince of Wales's visits to the house. Local gossip had it that the owners, finding the expense of the royal visits becoming more and more onerous, decided it might be cheaper to burn the house down. Whatever the truth, the beautiful house, built in 1742, was left a blackened shell. Two conservatories, which survived the fire, fell into disrepair and are only now being restored.

gineers and architects from any enthusiasm for developing freely and logically the techniques evolved by Paxton and his predecessors.

In the 1880s, the English Arts and Crafts movement gave expression to a romantic hostility to the machine and a strong feeling that any sort of mechanization epitomized the soullessness of modern life. Nor was the conservatory helped by the considerable changes in the social structure at the beginning of the twentieth century. The privileged echelons of English society enjoyed less leisure time as their wealth became harder to conserve, and many had to take a more active role in the businesses and commerce which provided their incomes. At the same time, female emancipation began to take women away from gracious pursuits like the daily tending of their flowers.

The two world wars hastened the decline of the conservatory. The vital need for homegrown food encouraged interest in the cultivation of vegetables such as cabbages and potatoes rather than exotic fruits and plants of only decorative value. With little energy to heat them, and little labor to tend them, many fine plant collections were lost forever, and conservatories were seen as superfluous structures. Fine plants and trees, once so carefully gathered and nurtured, ended up on the compost heap or in garden bonfires.

For the grand conservatory, the beginning of the end was poignantly signaled by the destruction of the Great Stove at Chatsworth in 1920. During the grim years of the First World War it had remained neglected and unheated, and many of its plants had died. This, coupled with escalating maintenance costs, led to the Duke of Devonshire's decision to demolish it. It took five explosions before this great edifice, resilient to the last, was completely destroyed, and it is ironic that the final blast was initiated by Paxton's grandson, Charles Markham.

Now, more than half a century after that calamity—and many lesser ones—the conservatory is enjoying a dramatic revival. An undoubtable factor in this development is the romantic nostalgia that is evident in so many areas of style and living—from fashion to literature to food.

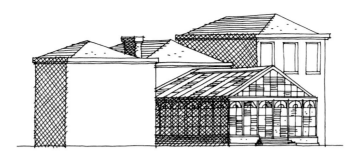

TRADITIONAL CONSERVATORIES

At the heart of every tradition is the wish to believe that nothing really changes. So it is with the traditional conservatory. It exists, in however diminished a scale, to show that its owner has the space and time available to set aside a living area dedicated to such simple, old-fashioned pleasures as sitting or walking among plants, chatting with friends, taking informal, unhurried meals, being at leisure.

Any utilitarian domestic purpose is secondary; the best traditional conservatories are firmly rooted in nostalgia. Their style, architecture, and arrangement reflect an affection for the past and a conscious and deeply felt wish to retain a sense of continuity.

Restored conservatories achieve their romantic effects naturally. They are embellished with scrolled, even crumbling, ironwork, glazed with old, flawed glass, hung with decorative brackets and replicas of gas lamps. Flaking paint and ancient, rimed clay pots only add to the nostalgic effect.

On the other hand, reproductions of Victorian conservatories suffer at first from being too perfect, their paint too fresh, their glass too clear. But after a year or two of natural weathering and jungly planting, they too can supply the desired effect of nonchalant profusion, while modern double glazing and heating systems prevent the drafts and drips that are often less charming aspects of a Victorian structure.

LEFT: One of the central attractions of that showplace of Art Deco, the Paris Exhibition of 1925, this delicately framed wrought iron and glass conservatory was recently bought as scrap metal and restored in Münster, West Germany.

Folie de Grandeur

"Frantic ingenuity . . . Victorian hubris"—Harlaxton Manor, near Grantham, Lincolnshire, has been variously praised and pilloried, and there is no doubt that it was a *folie de grandeur*, but the University of Evansville in Indiana, which now owns this noble pile, is perfectly content with it. Gregory Gregory, the eccentric nineteenth-century bachelor who commissioned the building, was not remarkably rich, as richness went in those days, but it is certain that he put all his available capital into creating this architectural extravaganza, said to be "his amusement, as hunting or shooting or feasting may be the objects of other people." Construction started in 1832 under the direction of Mr. Gregory and his architect, later to be replaced by another when their volatile patron decided that neo-Elizabethan could comfortably be combined with a touch of gargantuan baroque. Gregory Gregory had no dependants, and eventually, after various distant relatives had become squires of Harlaxton, the lease was acquired by the college. The building now serves as a residence for about 160 students who are taking courses abroad.

ABOVE: The entrance to Harlaxton is guarded by an appropriately Gothic gatehouse.

RIGHT: One of the first priorities of the University of Evansville was the restoration of the magnificent conservatory. New glass and glazing bars were installed, and stocks of plants were donated by many individuals as well as the Botanic Gardens at Kew and the Citrus Institute of Florida Southern College.

LEFT: A conservatory with a prefabricated ogee, or peaked variation of a dome, is attached to an American Colonial house in Connecticut.

LEFT: The triple-domed conservatory of Dallam Tower, Milnthorpe, is in Kendal in the English Lake District.

LEFT: Gently peaked, this conservatory at Blagdon House, in Witley, Surrey, is surrounded by a low stone balustrade. Modeled on the Crystal Palace, it is in fact only twenty-five to thirty years old. An unusual feature is the natural well which bubbles inside.

RIGHT: In Norbury Park, England, a stone-fronted conservatory is crowned with a gently curved glass dome.

RIGHT: A crested-dome conservatory sits between two orangeries at the Château Tourlaville, France.

RIGHT: Built in the Loudon style in the 1890s, this lovely iron-framed structure was leaning wildly to one side when the present owners bought it. Quotations for its repair were so high that a less costly winching and buttressing effort was decided upon. Now, several years later, the building remains stable and waterproof, and only the occasional replacement of the old lead glazing clips (which hold the glass in the frame) is necessary.

LEFT: Curved glazing bars and a peaked corner add romance to what would otherwise be a plain glazed extension. The gray enameled glazing bars give an impression of brightness and lightness, contrasting with the deep red tile-hung gables.

LEFT: This pretty double-aspect Victorian reproduction greenhouse is used to grow luscious out-of-season tomatoes and less practical jasmine.

LEFT: With its crested topknot and decorative square panes with roundel inserts, this particularly splendid Victorian conservatory is one of the great assets of a lovely National Trust manor house in North Wales.

RIGHT: Attached to a four-hundred-year-old Norfolk house, part of which is a converted barn, this conservatory was recently completely restored. The planting has recovered well; against the "warm wall" between the conservatory and the house, a beech tree, two grapevines, and peach and orange trees survive happily in spite of the lack of any supplementary heating. Tree begonias, fuchsias, and geraniums also flourish.

RIGHT: A custom-built conservatory designed by William Dunster has a brick plinth to link it naturally with the brick wall of the 1950s house.

RIGHT: The home of the Tempest family since Elizabethan times, Broughton Hall near Skipton, Yorkshire, is set in a famous Italian-style garden designed by William Andrews Nesfield, the nineteenth-century landscape architect of Regent's and St. James's parks in London. He also designed the low retaining wall and the nearby parterre of clipped box hedging in the Renaissance style. The lovely conservatory was designed by Bradford architects Andrews and Delaunay.

LEFT AND RIGHT: In some climates, while light is welcomed into the house, more heat is not. Here, near the coast in the south of France, narrow panes of glass in strong wooden framing admit a soft radiance while shutting out the blinding rays of the sun. From the outside the house looks cool and inviting.

LEFT: Although Paxton's Great Conservatory at Chatsworth was one of the most famous glass buildings in the world, it was just one among many other plant houses, camellia houses, and orangeries on the estate that were evidence of the Duke of Devonshire's lifelong interest in horticulture. This "conservatory wall," built in 1848, is one of the few that survived. Two rare camellia shrubs, which Joseph Paxton himself planted in 1850, still bloom.

LEFT AND RIGHT: Slender glazing bars of white-painted cedar give a light and lovely effect to this addition to a landmark Queen Anne house in Mersham, near Ashford, Kent. Built about thirty-five years ago as a camellia house, the conservatory still contains many of the original plants, mostly in shades of pink. They are prettily complemented by the pinkish brick floor, which was imported from a French brickworks. The owners of Stone Green Hall run it partly as a small country hotel and restaurant, and often serve summer meals among the camellias to their delighted guests.

RIGHT AND BELOW RIGHT: The amusingly asymmetrical facade of this English farmhouse used to present a blank face to the garden. Architect David Garbutt designed the conservatory so that its crested roof lines up exactly with the junction of the two gables. The conservatory base was built of brick to conform to the house, and the arched, wood-framed windows were sunk below the brick line to keep the effect light. Mechanical ventilators in the roof are thermostatically controlled, and conventional radiators supply heat that can be supplemented with an electrical system when necessary.

Colored glass panels make pretty patterns of light, and an old Brighton lamppost forms a central column.

LEFT AND BELOW LEFT: Unlike so many Victorian conservatories, this lovely example is contemporary with the house, which was built in 1856. An unusual feature is the back wall —made of some type of pumice or lava stone—obviously designed as a wet wall for ferns and rock plants. The conservatory was run-down and mostly glassless when the present owners bought it, and little plant life remained. Now, with the glass replaced and a waterfall running down the wall into a goldfish pond below, several dormant plants have been restored to health.

ABOVE, LEFT, AND BELOW LEFT: This north London house was built in 1852, but the conservatory is a later addition, possibly dating from the turn of the century. Most of its original fittings survive, including an intricately patterned mosaic floor, a built-in birdcage in one corner, and waist-high shelving with practical, lead-lined plant trays. The space is left unheated and used as a sitting room in the summer, when it is full of geraniums and pelargoniums; black grapes hang overhead.

ABOVE AND RIGHT: Not many houses in London have gardens that actually slope right down to the Thames riverbank; this is one of the few that do, so it seems odd that the previous owners had built an ugly potting shed in front of it. However, this was rapidly put right by the new owners, who replaced it with a charmingly small conservatory designed in the classic nineteenth-century style by Marston Langinger of Norfolk. It is built of treated and painted pine, and the detailing—decorative moldings, slim glazing bars, and cast metal braces—is elegant. Only 12 feet long by 8 feet wide, the conservatory shelters a richness of exotic plants, including orange columnea, fragrant jasmine, oleander, hibiscus, plumbago, bougainvillea, and geraniums.

Eiffel's Observatory

Several years ago Parisian architects François and Martine Hacq learned that the French Academy of Sciences was planning to sell for scrap metal a broken-down observatory dome built by Gustave Eiffel, the great nineteenth-century engineer who designed Paris's landmark tower. The Hacqs put in a bid, and soon found themselves the owners of a 15-foot metal cupola and its four iron supports. Their second stroke of luck was in finding a building site in the Heudon district, directly overlooking the Eiffel Tower. The architectural challenge was to find a way of incorporating a rare example of nineteenth-century scientific design with a modern house. Their solution was to cap the house with the observatory, yet keep them fairly separate from each other. The house sits between the supporting legs of the dome, which from one side overlooks Paris and, of course, the tower. Beneath the cupola is the kitchen/dining room, in front of which a terrace was built to take further advantage of the view. The Hacqs restored the dome to its original purpose, even re-creating its simple hydraulic system—it floats in a bowl of water, which is manually refilled from time to time. There is no sensible reason for owning this observatory dome, say the owners. It's impractical, and impossible to heat . . . but very poetic!

ABOVE LEFT: The front entrance shows the dome straddling the house.

CENTER LEFT: Through Eiffel's dome, there is a wonderful view of the Eiffel Tower in the distance.

LEFT: The back view of the house is a more conventional one.

RIGHT: Here, an exterior view of a unique and romantic house based on a romantic idea.

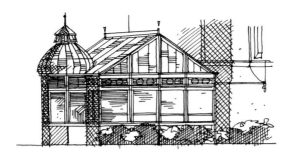

FUNCTIONAL CONSERVATORIES

Ownership of a conservatory does not necessarily signal a passionate interest in botany. And although nostalgia may play some part in the contemporary homeowner's decision to build an extension of glass rather than of brick or wood, a conservatory does have some entirely functional advantages over more solid constructions. A conservatory extension can provide a very flexible solution to the problem of achieving a comfortable balance between the lighting, heating, and ventilation of living spaces.

As a living room, for instance, the conservatory offers a light, relaxing, and informal retreat. Neo-Victorian shapes with rounded or polygon ends make interesting rooms and force original arrangements of furniture. If it is thoughtfully decorated, a glass living room can be as attractive in the winter as in the summer.

Warm colors, soft cushions, and friendly furniture like Lloyd loom chairs, sofas, and tables will look much more welcoming in winter than glass and metal furniture. Wooden slatted blinds can turn the cold gray light into an almost warm glow, and are useful in summer as well to deflect harsh midday sunlight and cast thin, evocative shadows across the room. Abundant displays of greenery, winter flowers, and baskets of hardy plants in a glazed living room are a marvelous way to offset bleak outdoor views. In summer,

LEFT: Much of this double-height dining room extension was built by the owners. Budget considerations led to their using opaque glass tiles in the roof and strong, load-bearing pine framing.

conservatory plants create an interesting middle ground between the main house and the garden, bringing another perspective to the home.

Double glazing will probably be needed to supplement normal heating in the winter. In the summer, however, a conservatory living room becomes a glorious sun-trap, needing only to be cooled by open doors. It is a particularly delightful place to be in the cool of the evening after a blazing day.

In the early nineteenth century, hostesses of a conservatory/dining room gained social points if their guests could reach behind their chairs to pluck an exotic orange from a nearby tree. Today, a conservatory used as a dining room can still provide a unique sense of theater, with candlelight flickering in double image against the glass and flowers such as tobacco plant (*Nicotiana*) or night-scented jasmine adding a heady fragrance.

The idea of an office in a conservatory has a positively bohemian attraction, perhaps because studios, which are for the most part glazed, have always been natural habitats for artists and photographers.

Apart from the obvious benefits of light and sun, a view of garden and sky and the sense of freedom that a glass wall provides help to lessen the feeling of being deskbound. As an office or workplace, a conservatory should, nevertheless, have a fair proportion of solid wall to provide support for shelves, workbenches, pictures, and bulletin boards, and to hold lighting fixtures for nighttime or close work. A workplace conservatory will probably need auxiliary heating; electric convection heaters are better than gas, as they create less condensation. The joints between glass and metal should be well sealed against dampness; although a few drips in a greenhouse simply add to its authentic charm, a desk full of smudged, damp papers is not acceptable in the average workroom.

Installing your bathroom in a conservatory is more practical than it sounds. The obvious implications of lack of privacy can be easily overcome, and there is nothing more luxurious than lying in the bath watching the clouds overhead or the wind-nudged leaves outside. If the bathroom conservatory is on the top

floor with nothing overlooking it except the occasional supersonic jet, a great proportion of the roof glass can be left unadorned. The sides, if they can be seen by neighbors, can be swagged in translucent cotton fabric which will let in the light but frustrate Peeping Toms. Opaque glass is a less attractive solution. Privacy on the ground floor is a little harder to obtain. One solution is to plant a tiny garden in front of the conservatory, so that a plant-clad wall blocks the outside view. In bathroom and pool enclosures, condensation does become a problem when steam meets glass, so air-conditioning of some sort is necessary if the room is not to become a year-round sauna. Since many plants thrive in a warm, steamy temperature, a glass bathroom is a lovely excuse to plan a tropical greenhouse. As indoor pools become more of a standard fixture than a luxury, it is almost common practice to enclose them in glass. With passive solar energy to warm the water, and glass to open up the outside world, family and friends can swim in warmth and comfort.

Stained glass panels fitted into the roof and walls create brightly colored reflections dancing on the surface of the pool water.

The scale of the space means you can be bold with plants; bring in large evergreen shrubs or small trees, build a rockery complete with ferns, moss, and fountain. To entertain those who come, in the Georgian phrase, to "take the waters," you could add a sauna, a Jacuzzi or spa pool, and, if you have the space, an elegant anteroom furnished with wicker chairs.

A conservatory is not an immediately obvious choice for a bedroom. It would be impractical and complicated to curtain a glass shell, roof and all, quite apart from the difficulties of maintaining an even day and night temperature. However, the idea of being able to gaze up at the stars each night while lying in bed appeals to some in a way that easily offsets the practical problems. Adding three glass walls to a bedroom extension is often a happy compromise with privacy in return for warmth, light, and a stunning panoramic view.

RIGHT AND BELOW RIGHT: A sympathetic addition to a typical London terraced house, this conservatory was designed by Colin Childerley and built by Alexander Bartholomew. Inside, the comfortable 1930s chairs and starburst rug create a conventionally pleasant room until you take the roof and end wall into account. The glazed triangular roof panels give way to solid wood at the "living" end, and all the framing is painted with a wood preservative incorporating a scarlet pigment.

FAR RIGHT AND BELOW FAR RIGHT: Careful detailing helps this conservatory fit in beautifully with the Edwardian house. Glazing bars are strong and simple, and the brick and wood-planked interior is painted white. Cast iron drainage grilles are sunk into the quarry tile floor; the clerestory is crowned with a dramatic roof crest. Apricot and peach trees grow along the warm inside wall.

41

Living Rooms

Glassed-in areas convert living rooms into relaxing, often more informal retreats.

LEFT: A glass verandah, which was added to the terrace of this turn-of-the-century French villa, serves as a warm, light-filled extension in the winter, and when the sliding doors are opened wide, a lovely transitional room between house and garden in the summer. Amusing objets trouvés add character, and the soft, cool color scheme counteracts the blazing Provencal sunlight.

BELOW LEFT: High-tech glass, concrete, and steel dominate in spite of their surface coldness. An open fire adds extra warmth in winter and proves there's nothing more efficient for roasting chestnuts.

RIGHT: Exposed beams are part of the decorative features of this modern German conservatory. The richness of the Oriental rug adds color and warmth to the slate floor, and the wood-burning stove makes a cheerful focal point on winter days.

ABOVE AND LEFT: The living space of this house on the edge of the Golzheim artists' colony in Düsseldorf, Germany, was doubled when the owners simply glassed in their patio. In the summer, old climbing roses and a twenty-year-old wisteria, which miraculously survived the building operations, provide natural shade and help blur the distinction between indoors and out. Winter warmth is provided by electric cables in the floor; in summer, extra ventilation is achieved by sliding back the glass panels in the walls and opening the room to the garden. Casual, comfortable furniture is made of materials that reemphasize the indoor-outdoor merger. A sofa and wicker chairs are at one end of the room, Bauhaus chairs and a wicker side table at the other. The glazed extension leads naturally onto a patio built from old paving and curb stones rescued from a local repair site.

LEFT: *Built in Brussels in the 1930s by an admirer of Le Corbusier, this house retained its purity and simplicity of line on the outside, but the interior was spoiled by years of inconsistent redecorating and rebuilding. Architect-designer Jean Jacques Hervy saw his chance to free the house from its clutter and restore it to its original style and lightness. This was achieved mainly by extensive glazing, bare wood floors, and glass bricks. Column tables are in the Italian Renaissance style; the rattan armchairs are from the 1930s.*

LEFT: *Modern art and Portuguese jars add to the eclectic style.*

LEFT: *The chestnut parquet flooring was restored to its original state but left untreated.*

RIGHT: *Glass bricks in the ceiling of the rear first-floor extension provide light underfoot in the second-floor recreation room. The "wink" chairs, a Toshiyuki Kito design, have folding Mickey Mouse ears and removable covers for a change of mood.*

ABOVE AND LEFT: This rooftop aerie was built over a vast warehouse. Architects Douglas Peix and William Crawford left the original skylight frame intact, but added frosted glass at eye level for privacy. Eventually a garden will be established on the deck high above the city streets.

ABOVE AND RIGHT: The extension beyond the columns in this Bridge-hampton, New York, house was formerly a screened verandah. The glazed section of the new roof lets in extra sunlight during the day and at night allows the owner to lie on the banquette and contemplate the stars. Architect: Christopher Owen.

ABOVE: *A modern porch was built onto an ancient French building of noble aspect simply to protect its entrance from wind and rain. Glass, steel, and ceramic tiles live companionably with the old brick walls.*

RIGHT: *Astonishingly, this California house measures only 20 × 20 × 40 feet, but architect Stephen Erlich's innovative use of glass and the soft pastel colors of the furnishings together give a remarkable feeling of space and light.*

Kitchens and Dining Rooms

In theory at least, a plant-filled kitchen eases the routine of preparing meals, and a profusion of plants can make a theatrical backdrop for dining under glass.

LEFT AND BELOW LEFT: When this French house was restored, high technology ruled in the design for a sparkling kitchen extension. Black-and-white was selected as the basic color scheme, to be relieved only by the natural green of the outdoor planting. Slim radiators under the windows control the temperature, and linen blinds control the light.

ABOVE RIGHT AND RIGHT: An extravagantly large space has been given up to the exotic sunken garden beside the dining area in a modern American condominium apartment. The steamy glass and soft, romantic look of the eating area contrast with the shipshape efficiency of the wood-lined, marble-topped galley kitchen.

RIGHT: All the cold surfaces in this extension—marble, granite, and mosaic—are gentled by the cheerful reds of the glazing bars and the beaded Art Deco lampshade.

LEFT: A Parisian journalist and antique collector had this conservatory built very cheaply and then added style and charm with flea market finds like the ceramic jardinieres, the pieces of old lace, and the bamboo furniture. The portemanteau now holds ferns and creepers instead of hats and coats.

LEFT: In one corner of a small paved garden, a sunroom opens on both sides to give a tent or pavilion effect.

LEFT: Victorian furniture is not entirely practical in a conservatory, but it makes an unexpectedly charming contrast with the quarry tile floor and white enameled glazing bars.

RIGHT: This very formal dining room makes no concession at all to standard conservatory furnishings. Chandelier, upholstery, and curtains are delightfully unrelated to their glass, stone, and brick surroundings.

LEFT: *Exterior blinds help keep this English kitchen cool in the heat of summer. The sympathetic use of wood, together with the plants, provides a cheerful mood and offsets the hard surfaces of tile and glass. Architects: Hunt-Thompson Associates.*

LEFT AND RIGHT: *Two glass facades, one double height, comprise a family living/kitchen extension in France designed by architect Estelle Lugat Thièbe. A wide concrete drain that takes rainwater from the steep roof forms a practical divider. White tiles and natural wood are the main design elements of the kitchen. The copper basin encourages the owner's small children to wash their hands.*

ABOVE AND RIGHT: *Perfect as they are for a typical English high tea, neither of these charming conservatories is as old as appearance suggests. A handmade lace tablecloth and ancient wicker chairs and lichen-covered bricks and old stained glass give both rooms a gentle mood of the nineteenth century.*

LEFT AND BELOW LEFT: *A set of Victorian barley twist drainpipes was the unlikely inspiration for this original conservatory in a London house. Stippled red and gilded, the pipes now serve as strong, highly decorative supports for the prefabricated roof. The glazing bars were painted red to match. Less a plant room than a striking dining room, the area is carpeted in gray to coordinate with the upholstery and the stippled and marbleized wood finishes.*

RIGHT: *Even the tiniest conservatory extension needs only one or two romantic elements to add charm and a feeling of space. Handmade quarry tiles, antique chairs, and a century-old tablecloth make this standard prefabricated conservatory by Francis Machin the perfect setting for diner à deux.*

LEFT AND RIGHT: *As the designer/ owner of this dining room conservatory says, once you've become used to eating "out" almost all year round, you can never imagine not having a glass extension to your living spaces. The two-story conservatory design resulted from the unexpected discovery, in a neighbor's garden, of the remains of an Edwardian spiral staircase buried among the hydrangeas. The staircase is built of old floor grilles salvaged from a demolished church; its handrail was not among the excavated sections, but was made up to match in steel, which was first zinc-coated against rust, then stove-enameled in white. Except for the aluminum supports, the entire main structure is wood-framed. When the conservatory was first built, the owners, plant lovers but not experts, filled it with as many plants and cuttings as they could. The following year they found themselves hacking their way out of a jungle which included twelve-foot-high sunflowers. Subsequently, they adopted a more conservative planting policy which produced the restrained profusion shown here: geraniums and pelargoniums, winter jasmine and plumbago, and a Black Hamburg grapevine that in three years grew twenty feet long and provided about forty pounds of delicious fruit.*

LEFT: Sculptor-painter Tom Merrifield's studio runs across the top floor of his London house, which also accommodates an art gallery run by his wife, Blackie. The contemporary breakfast/dining room leads off the narrow ship's galley kitchen, and here plants compete for attention with the antique "bits" that Blackie loves to collect, such as lace-trimmed cloths. One of them covers the ironing board, making it a handy sideboard when the Merrifields entertain, something they do often in this pretty room. The 1930s lamp was discovered in Aberdeen, Scotland, and became theirs in return for one of Tom's paintings. Each armchair around the table is different, chairs being another of Blackie's collecting passions. Evening dinner parties are held in candlelight as well as in the glow of Christmas lights, which once put up "were too lovely to take down."

RIGHT: A grownup's tree house was what Manhattan architect Richard Dattner designed as a winter/summer vacation retreat. Although the basic house shape is triangular, the curved greenhouse dining room softens the strong lines of the exterior and allows the pool, the visual core of the house, to add drama to dining at night, when it becomes a "shimmering grotto" of subdued light.

RIGHT: An almost impossibly tiny kitchen in a Paris suburb was imaginatively extended by the glass enclosure of a balcony beside it. Little more than a three-sided counter because of the roof angle that the space dictated, this small extra area has turned a functional kitchen into a friendly family room.

LEFT: Color and light combine in a lovely dining area on the roof of a New York apartment. Robert A. M. Stern was the architect.

BELOW LEFT: On the grounds of the great Castle Howard in Yorkshire, England, stands a more modest dwelling, "The Dairies," which in the nineteenth century was converted from its original purpose to a home for the estate's agent. Recent renovations included this magnificent garden room, built in a basic tomato-house (lean-to) style. The unpainted plaster walls contrast with the careful detailing of the huge pine worktable, which is painted with trompe l'oeil plans, maps, and letters. The three oval-topped Victorian windows, bought at a junkyard for a few pounds about forty years ago, provide a permanent view into an adjacent tropical hothouse. The treillage ceiling admits a cool, soft light into this lovely room.

RIGHT: Wine writer Hugh Johnson has, appropriately, a statue of Bacchus in his conservatory. A Greek Classical Revival marble (Athens, 1840), it shows him holding aloft a bunch of grapes, attended by a leopard at his feet. Cedar blinds shade this pretty conservatory, a simple but beautifully detailed lean-to which was added to the late-seventeenth-century house only six years ago. Plumbago and passionflower vines are beginning to clamber toward the ceiling. Other plants include daisies, fuchsias, pelargoniums, and lemons.

Studios and Workrooms

A room with a view can provide a serene atmosphere in which to work and even inspire creativity.

LEFT: Cotton canvas blinds above and split cane ones on the east-facing windows shield this home office from the brilliance of high summer.

RIGHT: Dutch architect Koen Van Velsen prefers overhead light on his drawing board and has softened the side light by installing opaque glass in the sliding panels, producing a shoji screen effect.

BELOW: At mezzanine level a drawing office borrows light from the double height conservatory below.

LEFT: A vaulted greenhouse provides even north light, the quarry tile floor tolerates paint drips, and the opaque roof softens the light, making this the perfect artist's studio.

BELOW LEFT: In an architect's home office, glass walls provide cool even light and a rooftop view of Berlin.

RIGHT AND BELOW RIGHT: A Sunday painter's studio and office in one of the English southern counties began as a simple loft extension to a garage. Architect Maxim Benthall extended his brief to provide a pyramid conservatory with a view over the nearby park. In a curious combination of rustic and modern styles, he used solid oak tree trunks embedded in concrete as supports.

LEFT: In lower Manhattan, a sun space serves as a film director's study. A unity of colors and materials adds to the visual space of what is really a small room. Bleached decking is used as a continuous surface material, extending the wall and the planked seating onto the open terrace. A mirrored section inset above the wall reflects the glazing bars, giving an impression of infinite space beyond. Architects: Shelton, Mindel.

Bathrooms and Bedrooms

Away from public view, a conservatory bathroom or bedroom can be both practical and beautiful.

Privacy was not a problem when architect Christopher Owen planned this marvelous glass-enclosed penthouse in New York City. Birds are the only passersby at this height, so the owners can enjoy the splendor of uninterrupted views all around.

TOP: Part of the terrace has been left unenclosed for summer living.

ABOVE: One bedroom door leads to the greenhouse, the other opens to the terrace, depending on the season.

RIGHT: Across the Central Park reservoir is a stunning view of the Manhattan skyline.

LEFT AND CENTER LEFT: *In the white marble bathroom of the penthouse shown on the previous page, a mirror wall doubles the effect of the view. Sunbathing is an after-the-bath pleasure all year round.*

BOTTOM LEFT: *Even when the roof slope is as steep as this one, a bath can be comfortably accommodated within its angle.*

RIGHT: *Fine-tuned temperature control whatever the season was the main requirement of the owners of this Parisian bedroom/bathroom suite. In winter, the white canvas ceiling blinds are pulled back and the open fireplace is lit. In summer, blinds shade the room while a ceiling fan cools it.*

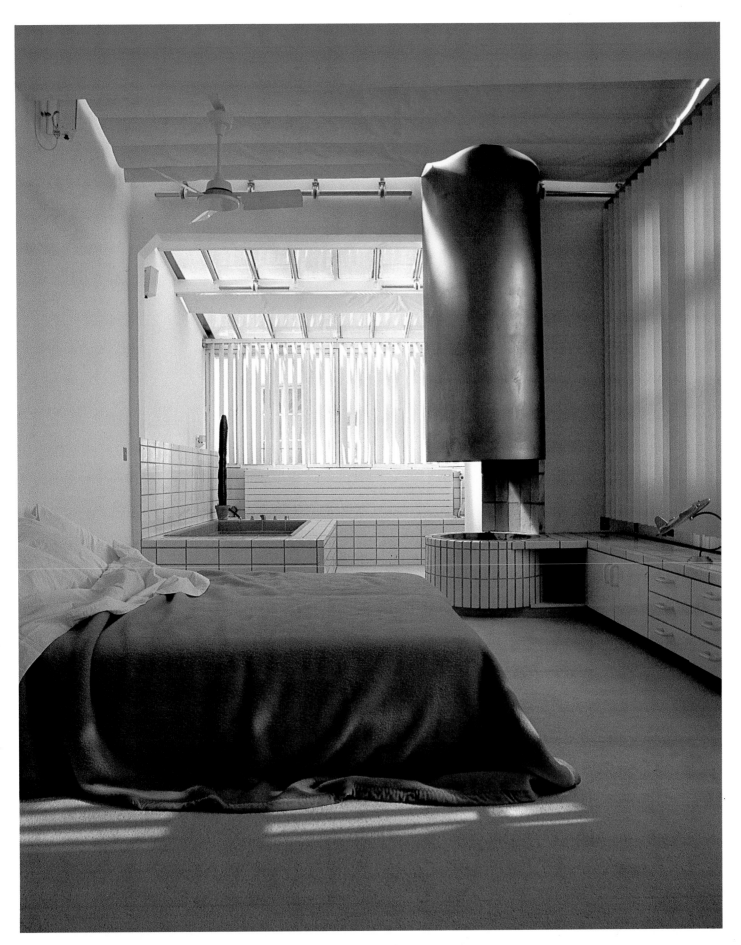

Pool Rooms

Glazed pool enclosures provide warmth and humidity for plants and a glamorous setting for twenty laps a day.

LEFT: A family bathroom, pool, and recreation area enclosed in a curved glass extension leads off a sauna and small gymnasium. Opposite the pool a long tiled wall is separated by columns into niches containing washbasins and shallow storage. A bidet and WC are separated from the main room by half-height walls in white tile, but otherwise the whole room provides a pleasantly relaxing and health-oriented center for family life.

ABOVE: Within a large garden, a peaked glass dome sections off a spa/pool area which has become a miniature jungle. The heat and steam combined keep the exotic plants flourishing even during an East Coast winter, and the owners can enjoy a tropical holiday from real life every time they step into their tiled pool.

79

TOP AND ABOVE: *Although physically attached to the main house by walls and an enclosed passageway, this pavilion and its bathhouse wing in Greenwich, Connecticut, seem completely separate. The postmodern design by architect Robert A. M. Stern was in response to the owner's request for a structural pavilion where art would precede function. The remarkable result is this billowing glass-shingled tent which is lit by natural light from above and in the summer can be opened out to the landscape. Together with the screened porch at one end it provides a huge entertaining/living space.*

RIGHT: *Brass-stemmed palm trees, dazzling colors, and mosaic tiles add to the pharaonic grandeur.*

LEFT: A wood-burning stove-fireplace at the end of this pool holds promise of reward for effort, although the ogee-framed roof helps maintain a reasonably sybaritic temperature.

BELOW LEFT: An opaque glazed roof filters the midsummer sun in this French pool, leaving a cooling view of the atrium garden beside it.

RIGHT: Reflections on a summer afternoon in England: the intricately glazed dome houses both a pool and the perfect place for strawberry-and-cream teas.

LEFT AND CENTER LEFT: The small carriage house attached to this farmhouse in Washington, D.C., was so dilapidated the owners considered destroying it. Instead, they rebuilt it to contain a sauna and casual living area and then added the glazed pool enclosure in a complementary style. Architect Winthrop Faulkner designed the 55 × 12-foot lap pool with a whirlpool at one end. Solar panels on one side help maintain a pleasant temperature, and a basement underneath the carriage house contains the filtration and heating equipment.

BOTTOM LEFT: Dogs play an important part in the life of the German painter who owns this pool house, which was formerly a stable. The atmosphere is kept at a tropical temperature for the sake of the exotic plants. Over it all, a statue of Echo, a favorite pet, stands guard.

RIGHT: Stained glass insets give an ecclesiastical feeling to this beautiful pool house in Somerset, England. Appropriately, it is attached to a former Victorian vicarage. The grapevine growing happily under the roof announces harvest time by dropping grapes into the hexagonal pool, changing the water to a pale pink. Both the house and the living/dining area beyond the pool were designed by Martha Johnson.

ABOVE: A highly individualistic clover-leaf-shaped pool is enclosed within an ogee-roofed structure designed by Francis Machin.

LEFT: A modern double-arched conservatory encloses a pool and a sitting room to make a stunning area for summer entertaining.

RIGHT: At one end a grotto disguises the housing for the heating and filtration equipment. York stone slabs surround the pool, which is tiled with colored mosaic.

Small-Budget Extensions

Ingenious use of even the smallest spaces, perhaps just the deepening of a window embrasure, can create the atmosphere of a garden for relatively small expense.

LEFT: Azaleas frame a city view in a reading niche created by the installation of a prefabricated section of curved metal glazing bars.

LEFT: A collection of shells, miniature cacti, and other natural objects links this interior with the lush outdoors.

RIGHT: Heavy black glazing bars match the geometric style of this contemporary French house.

RIGHT: In the private courtyard of a Parisian suburban redevelopment, a narrow building gains light and drama from a stepped glass extension framed in sea-green wood.

RIGHT: In a narrow space between two terraced houses, a restored conservatory shelters a rich collection of ferns and flowering shrubs.

LEFT: A narrow gap gains drama from its double-height glass enclosure.

LEFT: Enclosed in glass, a derelict backyard space becomes a useful and pretty living area.

RIGHT AND BELOW RIGHT: This dual purpose guest/dressing room was once a tiny terrace next to the master bedroom. The fabric-covered ceiling and wall blinds made of Indian cotton transform a sunny corner into an intimate alcove. Architects: Shelton, Mindel Associates.

Rooftop, Porch, and Window Extensions

While it is true that one of the greatest advantages of a conservatory is that it can form a pleasant transition between a house and its garden, it is not the only way to enjoy the benefits of living under glass. A helicopter view of any major city will show the recent proliferation of small greenhouses high above the traffic and pollution of the city jungle. Some are simply glassed-in bay windows or porches; others stand on flat roof extensions or seem to have alighted like bubbles among the more prosaic central heating systems and elevator shaft machinery that decorate the average city roof. Whatever their size or position, they are an apartment dweller's way of reaching out a little into the environment. Sunlight, plants, and a nearer view of the sky bring a sense of freedom within the constrictions of multiple dwellings. In one American city recently, the sudden popularity of miniature greenhouses led to the civic authority's realization that many of them were being used for the cultivation of that exotic plant, cannabis. It seems that law enforcement agents take the view that people who live in glass houses shouldn't get stoned.

TOP LEFT: Against ivy-clad walls, a green-framed second-floor garden room encloses a stone balustrade.

LEFT: In early-morning sunlight a white-framed conservatory sparkles against glowing red walls.

LEFT: Three ogee-roofed conservatories are in a small row of London houses. Two are at ground level and one is perched high.

RIGHT: Glass houses at unexpected levels enliven a cityscape.

 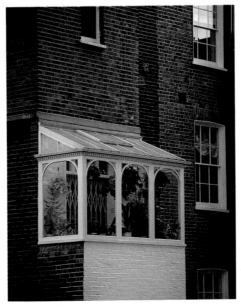 

Parlor Gardens

Collecting was a mania with middle-class Victorians. Shells, beads, dried flowers, scrap pictures, decorative pins, stuffed birds—anything that could be framed, arranged, displayed on stands, or immortalized under glass added to the charm and clutter of the Victorian parlor. Plants did not escape this trend, and during the second half of the nineteenth century a drawing room was considered incomplete without a Wardian case (see Nathaniel Ward, page 8) or an aquarium. Sometimes the planting was rather bizarre; gentle young Victorian misses apparently took delight in catching live flies to feed to carnivorous plants, such as the Venus flytrap or savage sundew.

Some Wardian cases were heated either by gas or, occasionally, with hot water pipes. Other models, as if in anticipation of the modern use of solar energy, were designed to trap and conserve sunlight.

Many were very pretty, with brass frames and colored glass insets. Some were rustic, built of plain slatted wood or of curved tree branches and twigs in fanciful free forms. Others were elaborately gilded, enameled, and medallioned. Yet others were absolutely hideous examples of the cabinetmaker's art carried to excess, with bulging cabriole legs, entwined cherubs, fish and animals, and an abundance of red plush velvet. The Crystal Palace reproduced in miniature was a popular shape which looked rather pleasing, but some families made firm statements about their wealth and status with Wardian cases that almost resembled Gothic cathedrals.

Of all the plants with which these parlor gardens (or "parlor pets," as they were nicknamed) were filled, ferns were by far the most popular. Ferns were even thought to have some mystical healing and soothing properties, and collectors searched farther and farther afield for more exotic varieties, as some botanists warned that rare species might disappear under this onslaught.

Historian and author Charles Kingsley issued a mild warning to fathers: "Your daughters perhaps, have been seized with the prevailing 'Pteridomania' and are collecting and buying ferns with Ward's cases wherein to keep them (for which you have to pay). . . ."

Today, modern versions of the Wardian cases are becoming popular, not just for their decorative value but for the same reason they were popular with Victorians—because the sealed container protects the delicate plants from pollution. Glass carboys, aquarium tanks, and large confectionery jars are among possible containers for modern bottle gardens. Tiny plants in well-sterilized and well-drained soil will grow for years with very little attention.

Many garden shops now sell elegant, already planted terrariums with metal-bound glass panels, often in fanciful shapes slightly reminiscent of their extravagant predecessors.

OPPOSITE, ABOVE LEFT: *Bottle gardens are the modern version of the Victorians' beloved terrariums.*

OPPOSITE, ABOVE RIGHT: *A typically popular shape, this early Wardian case was built to shelter a rich collection of mixed ferns.*

LEFT: *On a kitchen bench, a small portable greenhouse becomes a forcing house for herbs and seedlings.*

ABOVE RIGHT: *In one of the few remaining untouched Victorian houses in London, two of the bay windows have been glazed to provide miniature greenhouses. This one is edged with a decorative border of blue and white tiles. The house, in Kensington, was once the home of Punch cartoonist Edward Linley Sambourne.*

RIGHT: *A 1980s version of the Victorian window greenhouse, this pretty windowsill provides fresh herbs almost all year round.*

ABOVE AND RIGHT: *Conservation of birds rather than plants is the reason for this glazed unit in a spacious New York loft. Built against a wall of natural brick, it makes a superb central focus to the room and is an original use of a standard greenhouse extension specially adapted to provide adequate ventilation.*

MODERN CONSERVATORIES

Ever since the time of the Crystal Palace, glass has been associated with the most revolutionary developments in architecture. Paul Scheerbart, the visionary German architectural critic of the early years of this century, wrote that "glass brings us the new era; brick culture is a burden." Both he and his more Utopian-minded contemporaries saw the heavy masonry constructions of their day not simply as aesthetically undesirable, but also as embodying repressive and hostile values. Glass architecture, in contrast, to them represented the liberation of the human spirit and an environment in which love and harmony would more easily flourish.

Scheerbart's dream of all-glass buildings has come true in the second half of this century, though owing less to idealism than to the fact that radical innovations in glass technology have opened up far greater possibilities for glass construction. Sheets of glass can be made far stronger, so they no longer need the intricate webbing and support of heavy iron and steel frames. Insulating and reflecting layers can be built into the glass so that it diverts heat and glare during the day and actually helps to conserve heat at night. Other developments in heating and ventilating systems generally have all combined to make the construction of almost entirely glass dwellings a practical possibility rather than a charming folly.

LEFT: The asymmetrical curves of this stunningly modern conservatory are very much in sympathy with the style of the 1825 house. Architect: Jon Benson (assisted by Katerina Kyselkova).

There have been some intriguing and beautiful glass houses, like Mies van der Rohe's Farnsworth House, built in 1945–50 as a weekend retreat in an isolated woodland setting in Illinois. It was probably the first domestic house to be surrounded entirely by glass walls, which were framed by white-painted steel bars. It represented, both in its plain box shape and in the choice of materials, the ultimate expression of Mies's philosophy, "Less is more." Another similarly advanced building was that of the eclectic American architect Philip Johnson, who built his Glass House in New Canaan, Connecticut, in 1949. It was completely transparent except for the central bathroom cylinder.

The idea of all-glass dwellings, however, probably has a limited future, more to do with the geography of cities than with any limitations in the material itself. A glass house isolated in a forest or beside an ocean is obviously a far more attractive proposition than one adjoining a busy thoroughfare or on a site only yards from its neighbors. But the idea of a *partially* glazed section is becoming almost an accepted part of modern architectural design. It could therefore be said that conservatories have been the inspiration for many of the more sympathetic developments in recent domestic architecture.

There is a growing concern to find alternative energy sources as fuel and electricity become ever more expensive. Through the use of heat-absorbent glass, storage panels, and the other technical developments already mentioned, the heat which is attracted to conservatories and other large areas of glass can be channeled and conserved so as to warm houses almost all year round. Many modern architects see the house of the future as being centered inside a large covered courtyard, its south side comprising an enormous sloping window flanked by solar panels. At exhibitions of model homes, even some of the most conventional builders offer at least one design that incorporates a conservatory.

In the nineteenth century the conservatory represented traditional and cozy ideals of domestic harmony, the practical pursuit of leisure interests, and the joy of building beauty for beauty's sake. Strange though it may seem, these values are now playing a part in making the glass extension an important basis for the dwellings of the future.

RIGHT: Apartment dwellers gained access to the communal garden and a tiny sun space of their own by glazing a porch within cobalt blue enameled metal bars and adding a spiral staircase at the first-floor living room level. The sauna room in the cellar gained a protective roof and the second-floor bedroom a tiny balcony on the roof.

FAR RIGHT: Like the windows of the house, this neoclassical porch is framed in wide bars of white-painted wood but otherwise pays no heed to the style of the house itself, a typical suburban terraced one with no previous claim to distinction.

RIGHT: Instead of the more expected mock-Victorian conservatory addition, the owners of this semidetached London house chose a dramatic modern double extension. There are actually two conservatories, the upper one leading from the first-floor bathroom and the lower one forming a dining area next to the kitchen, with no interconnection.

FAR RIGHT: Another contradiction in glass, this extension has a curved roof and is guarded by rigidly disciplined sentinel trees. The porch opens up a formerly narrow front door, thus allowing light into the dark interior hall.

The Secret House with a Glass Lid

Beset by even more than the day-to-day problems architects face, Borek Sipek had to overcome the limitations of an extraordinarily difficult site tightly wedged between nondescript neighboring houses. Building regulations in Hamburg, Germany, required that the house be built at a right angle to the road, which was impossible to do. In order to give the appearance of complying with the regulations, Sipek built the visible part of the house as a peaked glass "lid" at a right angle to the road. Underneath it is the basic brick house, comfortably parallel to the road. While this solution may not have been one that the city authorities had in mind, Sipek's ingenuity produced a remarkable result.

The steel frame of the glass section was put in place with the cellar foundation so that it sits like a cage above the building. All the living rooms are downstairs. A clay wall is heated with gas so that it transmits warmth to the whole house, rather on the principle of a pottery kiln. Even without this supplementary heating, the glass top keeps the house very warm —in fact, sometimes too warm in summer in spite of side vents in the "lid," which open automatically when the house overheats (and close again if it rains). This problem too is being solved with ingenuity, though of a simpler kind: the owners have planted deciduous trees and creepers around the greenhouse. By next summer they will have natural shade from a canopy of leaves.

TOP LEFT: The glass "lid" looks especially striking between its conventional neighbors.

CENTER LEFT AND LEFT: The space provides a year-round sitting room under glass.

RIGHT: From the conventional part of the house, a staircase leads to the conservatory/attic.

LEFT: *Although it looks like the result of a single design effort, this hilltop house in New Jersey was partly reconstructed to an imaginative scheme by architect Robert A. M. Stern. Its glass center section shelters a new indoor pool.*

RIGHT: *This house has changed the personality of its owner. The vice-president of a steel company, he was surprised to realize that a year of living here in the woods of South Carolina had turned him into a nature lover. The glass walls, their views uninterrupted by any superfluous interior division, afford a closeness to nature that he had never before experienced. Because he was in the business, the owner asked that the house be framed with steel—something few people can afford. Architects Stephen Tilly and Alan Buchsbaum were delighted to have this opportunity, because steel can span larger spaces than the more usual wood beams, allowing them to provide a vast two-story living area. Even the stairs, joists, and grating are of steel, but the outer walls are of wood, both for its appearance and for its thermal insulation properties.*

RIGHT: *The wonderful folly of a glass tower on the left was completed only recently in Ascot, England, but the extension on the right is contemporary with the 1930s brick house behind. The octagonal tower is 21 feet high and contains a spiral staircase leading to the upper bedroom floor. It is glazed in toughened windshield glass as a special safety precaution because of icicles. Icicles? Apparently it isn't unknown for stratospherically formed icicles to fall from jet aircraft as they reduce their height. This owner does not want his glass folly to fall victim to a Damoclean icicle plunging from the evening Concorde as it comes in to roost at the airport nearby. Architect: Andrew Blenkinsop.*

ABOVE AND RIGHT: On the south facing side of this Bridgehampton, New York, home, a 20 × 30 × 5-foot solarium collects and absorbs the sun's rays to achieve, even on partially cloudy days, a temperature of 80°F. To help heat absorption and retention, the interior floor and walls are tiled with black quarry stones. French doors and windows open into all living spaces to allow circulation of the collected warm air. Design: Jeffrey Milstein for Barbara Brooks.

BELOW AND RIGHT: A development of five half-glassed houses was built around trees. Almost everything in the interiors is white, with occasional touches of black, and the living areas are separated from the glass fronts by split bamboo blinds painted white. At present these blinds protect the inhabitants against the glare, but eventually the glass extensions will be completely covered with climbing plants. Architect: Horst Schmitgens.

ABOVE AND LEFT: *The glass houses absorb the warmth of the setting sun while their conventional neighbors chill. White canvas blinds provide soft shade when necessary, and the house is so warm that marble floors are not incongruous even in a northern European climate.*

LEFT: *In a new top-floor addition to a house in a Paris suburb, the use of natural stained wood, indoors and out, adds a fresh Scandinavian feeling. Bernard Kohn was the architect of this house and the one below.*

BELOW: *Apart from the roof framing of aluminum, all other structural sections are of natural pine, slightly darkened with preservative, in this ground-level extension to an old house in Paris.*

RIGHT: Although it's possible the average Italian citizen of nearly two thousand years ago might not see the connection, this brave and astonishing design is in fact based on the ancient domus, the typical middle-class Roman house. As can be seen from excavations at Pompeii and Herculaneum, a domus was built around a vast hall (atrium) with an open roof (impluvium). Reception, living, and dining rooms opened onto the atria, and the outside walls of the house presented a closed and securely impenetrable face to the surrounding streets, just as this one does. Designed by the unconventional German architect Horst Schmitgens, this house has an entirely windowless exterior wrapped, like a huge parcel, with wide concrete corrugations that give it a soft, almost pneumatic appearance. Inside, however, it opens up to reveal its heart of glass. Brilliant white tiles and blue-painted metal framing make it look like an undersea city, an effect which is heightened by the shimmering reflections of the central pool.

ABOVE: The gleaming white floor of glazed German tiles and the strong red and black of the stove-enameled glazing bars help make a tiny Parisian conservatory seem more spacious. The yellow chair is a copy of the famous 1938 sling chair by Jorge Ferrari-Harboy.

ABOVE LEFT: Many glass extensions are built to trap sunlight; this one in East Hampton, New York, was planned as an escape from it. All the principal rooms in the house have superb ocean views, so the greenhouse was built on the north side as a shady retreat. The mezzanine balcony is a study leading from the master bedroom. All the wood surfaces, shown here in the bluish light of a blazing summer day, are in fact gray-stained cedar. Architects: Gwathmey, Siegel and Associates.

LEFT: A tiled catwalk links the stairs between two levels; it also has a passive solar energy function because heat is stored in the airspace between the insulating glass and the inner, heat-collecting wall of heavy masonry, which has been painted a rich earth red.

ABOVE RIGHT: Built on the foundation of a former terrace, this galvanized steel verandah is part of the range of prefabricated designs from a French supplier. The metal is simple to paint, needing one base coat of emulsion, one of gloss, and one top coat.

RIGHT: Two stories are sheathed in a sun-catching slanted wall of tinted glass framed in blue metal. Ventilation flaps at the top reduce the heat and condensation in midsummer, and a flower-filled balcony trims its edge.

A Piece of Glass Dropped into a Forest

This northern French country house reflects the light and shade of the trees that surround it. Before he began his design, architect Thomas Herzog took hundreds of photographs of every detail of the land and its woods and stream. He then built a series of *maquettes* to establish which design would intrude on as little of the environment as possible. He found his ideal shape in this series of energy-conserving wedges and his ideal material in glass.

LEFT AND LEFT BELOW: Whether their heavenly view is of scurrying clouds by night or dappled sunlight by day, the owners say they are hardly aware of the glass barrier between them and their surroundings.

RIGHT: A wooden walkway gives a Japanese feeling to this interior court, where the temperature seldom falls below 59°F, a perfect climate for dozens of warmth-loving plants.

BELOW RIGHT: Another small court-yard adjoins the dining area. Like the walkway, it is wood-planked, in contrast to the more traditional honey-colored tile floors throughout the rest of the house.

Civic Clearsightedness

Decades after the most imaginative American and European architects had shown how glass could transform the face of public buildings, even the most conservative city architects and town planners began to see its possibilities for state-owned housing developments.

In the last ten to fifteen years public funds have been used in many countries to build superbly functional and often highly innovative glasshouses for living in. People who live under glass naturally tend to look outward, so that an interest in and concern for the environment come more naturally to them than to people encased in solid walls. Therefore, private and public buildings made wholly or partly of glass frequently have rather more than average attractive surroundings.

ABOVE LEFT: Residents of this experimental 32-apartment development in southern Sweden (completed in 1981) find that they need auxiliary heat sources for about two months less than do their neighbors in ordinary houses. They also enjoy flowering plants and ripening tomatoes indoors, even while the first winter snows are shrouding the glass above.

LEFT: Another imaginative development has tiers of half-glazed townhouses built around a shopping center. At first glance, a Neapolitan hillside or perhaps a Mediterranean resort? In fact, it is in Bloomsbury, in the heart of London. Designed by Patrick Hodgkinson, it is known locally as The Greenhouse.

LEFT: A Parisian rooftop view, though not a usual one, was created by the renovation of a row of decaying houses. Shaded glass roofs and gables convert formerly shabby attics into dramatic ateliers high among the chimneys.

RIGHT: Skyscraping apartments become San Francisco sun spaces, as though the solid walls have peeled away on one corner to reveal the bright new glass skin beneath.

Solar Energy

The cost of gas, coal, and oil and the pollution they cause have increasingly focused attention on conservation and on alternative methods of heating buildings. Efficient insulation through the creation of a completely sealed and airtight house with mechanical ventilation is one approach.

Another is the development of ecologically sound forms of heating, such as the "heat heap," whereby the heat generated by the decomposition of a huge pile of wood chips in the garden is piped into the house. This system is currently being used by commercial greenhouse owners; every eighteen months or so they dig the wood compost back into the soil and start the system off once more with a new pile of chips.

But for the moment, the most obvious economical and generally accessible method of heating involves collecting the sun's radiant energy.

Double glazing, with a metallic coating on the outer facing sheet of glass, can trap solar energy to a much greater extent than other types of glazing, and can also retain warm air more successfully. As a means of exploiting this kind of solar heating, a conservatory has unique advantages. Obviously its efficiency depends on a number of factors, such as its size in relation to the rest of the house, the direction it faces, and the angle at which the glass is slanted. Ideally, the conservatory should face the sun or at least be within thirty to forty-five degrees of the sun's path. It is rather more difficult to work out the actual slant of the glass, since the angle of the sun itself varies from region to region and from season to season. The sharper the angle of the roof, the more the conservatory will benefit from low winter sun.

Collecting the sun's rays is only the first part of the solar energy process. What can turn an ordinary conservatory into a heat generator for the rest of the house is the efficient storage of collected heat. A storage medium that can absorb radiant energy when the sun is out will help to prevent overheating in a conservatory and at the same time allow heat to be slowly released when there is no sun. Without such a medium, temperatures within a glass room are liable to

fluctuate wildly. Water in containers is one simple form of storage. Another is the use of concrete, preferably both in the foundations of the conservatory and in the dividing wall between the conservatory and the main house.

Many conservatories use additionally a storage system employing eutectic salts, a chemical product which is a liquid by day and a solid heat-emitting source by night. The final requisite of domestic solar heating is an efficient distribution system, whereby the right amount of hot air is released inside the house during winter months and outside it in warm seasons. There are a number of ways in which this can be done, including manually and thermostatically controlled fans, and windows, doors, and vents.

Not only country dwellers and those with spacious gardens can take full advantage of the sun's energy. Greenhouses on the roofs of apartment buildings will become an ever more common feature of the urban landscape. Apart from providing the general benefits of conservatories, these structures can recycle the air from the exhaust vents of the buildings on which they stand, thus not only minimizing heat losses through roofs but also protecting the greater environment from pollution.

A conservatory is itself a passive form of solar heating. An active system employs solar panels that absorb the sun's heat and transfer it to water running in pipes behind them. A low-wattage pump is used to drive the water, although recently there have been experiments with solar panel systems without electronic parts.

Because the cost efficiency of solar heating depends on a careful balance between initial investment and recurrent expenses, and the specific installation and its purposes (for example, the proportion of heating to be taken from solar and from other supplementary sources), many of the technical aspects of it are not widely understood. It may be some time before solar heating as a basic system is universally accepted and used.

In the meantime, the domestic conservatory is likely to remain the most feasible and attractive way of partially storing solar heat.

RIGHT: Here is the typical basis of a modern solar heating system.

1 Orientation. Double-glazed walls can be orientated up to 30° east/west of south for maximum heat gain. Triple glazing can be further east/west of south.

2 Glazing. Vertical glazing allows maximum solar radiation into the conservatory in winter. Use double/triple/solar reflective glazing incorporated with thermal breaks in framing and good weather seals. Plastic materials can be used as roof glazing to prevent breakages. Doors should also have effective seals to prevent air leaks.

3 Blinds. To prevent heat loss through glass at night and to provide shade on hot summer days, window/roof blinds should be used.

4 High level ventilator. A thermostat controlled ventilator at high level will balance heat buildup in summer.

5 Heat absorption and direct radiation into house. Concrete/masonry wall and floor will absorb heat in day and re-radiate heat at colder periods (night) into the conservatory and adjacent rooms. Openings in this wall, which will allow heat into the house during the day, should be closed at night.

6 Greenhouse effect. Warmed air and re-radiated warmed air rises and is collected at a high level.

7 Solar air collection. Solar heated warm air can be collected into a high level manifold or duct and drawn directly into colder rooms or fan-pulled into a heat store.

8 Heat store. Masonry, or water-filled, insulated storage units store heat by day for redistribution at night.

9 Heat retrieval. A fan drawing heat into the store during the day can be reversed to extract the heat and recirculate it through the house at night.

THE CONSERVATORY IN DETAIL

Plants do furnish a room; a conservatory is a gratifying space to decorate, since plants provide a pleasingly theatrical setting for the other elements in it. Whatever the function of your conservatory, there is one major factor to take into consideration when choosing furniture and accessories; they must be reasonably tolerant of dampness. French-polished or waxed furniture will not survive even occasional accidental watering, nor will it like the heat of high summer. So unless you are prepared to move them out of the way every time you water, and cover them against the sun, wooden treasures are best left in adjoining rooms.

Chairs and tables, floors and shelf units, pots, plant stands, and brackets should have a natural look. Avoid the formal in favor of the whimsical; abandon the rococo for the slightly rustic. Materials such as cane, iron, stone, and brick are ideal. If wood is used, it should be durable, like teak, or finished with several layers of paint. Flowerpots should be clay and jardinieres ceramic—never plastic.

Victorian tiered plant stands can still be found. Some, which were designed as showy centerpieces for plants and ferns, are circular, rather like huge cake stands. Others are semicircular, to stand against a wall, or triangular, to fit into a corner. Modern reproductions of classic furniture and fittings are commonly available in aluminum.

LEFT: *Patterned on a Victorian original, this green-painted spiral staircase connects the two levels of a modern city conservatory, enclosing a bathroom, entrance hall, and summer sitting room.*

Furniture

The most acceptable chairs and sofas are made of willow, cane, teak, iron, or aluminum, but they tend to be uncomfortable without cushions or pads. Although chintzy, flowery fabrics are often thought of as suitable for conservatories, in fact plain fabrics like natural canvas look far better and do not compete for attention with the real flowers in the room.

Rattan cane furniture looks like bamboo but lacks its characteristic "joints." A type of comfortable, tub-shaped chair is often made in rattan, as well as a Chesterfield-type settee with a rolled back and arms.

Willow is a highly suitable material for conservatory furniture, but it does get scruffy rather quickly if it is left in its white, unpeeled state. It can be washed down with warm soapy water, but it is probably more practical to paint it (ideally a deep jungle green). A light honey gloss finish, achieved with a coat of medium varnish, is also attractive. The simplest style of willow chair is like a round upturned basket with a solid back.

The traditional wooden park bench type of seating comes in a variety of designs, of which the best are the plain, upright ones softened with cushions. Benches made of teak can be sealed or painted. A traditional French garden chair design is available in chestnut wood, split and woven like an old-fashioned strawberry basket. Folding wood and canvas directors' chairs are inexpensive and suitable for dining chairs in a conservatory, but you lean back in them at your own risk.

Wicker Lloyd Loom chairs are a good compromise between dining and armchairs and, prolific in their original dingy gold paint (they used to be standard seating in the picture palaces of the 1930s), they can still be found in junk shops. Repainted in sparkling primary colors or cool sherbet pastels, they are almost the ideal conservatory chairs.

Another more individualistic conservatory piece would be an antique "campaign" bed. It is usually made of

cast iron and webbed with steel straps, though the upholstery almost always needs replacing.

A conservatory table should have a really durable surface so that it continues to look good in spite of heat, sunlight, water, candle wax, and the occasional summer shower of French dressing. Slatted teak, iroko, and oak tables or Lloyd Loom wicker bases with glass tops are conventional choices. A marble or polished slate slab on a metal base makes a more original table.

In the end, though, the conservatory needs only the essentials to furnish it, for comfort or dining or whatever other purpose. Most well-planted conservatories need little extra embellishment.

ABOVE AND LEFT: The late Sir Cecil Beaton, the celebrated designer and photographer, loved the sense of theater that a conservatory can provide. Many of his famous photographs, especially fashion shots and portraits of women, were taken here, in the conservatory he added to his country house in 1962. Until his death in 1980, Sir Cecil used it regularly for serving predinner drinks; it was always kept lavishly stocked with flowering plants from the greenhouse outside. Furniture was chosen for elegance rather than comfort, as guests who have sat on his Chinese porcelain seats or reproduction Mackintosh chairs will testify. In the exterior view, Sir Cecil himself can be seen in the doorway of the house.

Plant Stands and Shelves

Planting benches can be made of hardwoods, galvanized metal, or whatever masonry is incorporated in the main structure of the conservatory itself. Galvanized pipe framing can be combined with steel mesh for the bench base itself; this is usually most successful when edged with a wooden lip to hide the practical but prosaic metal parts.

Decorative plant stands are easily found; wire Victorian reproductions are particularly suitable for traditional conservatories.

LEFT: In a conservatory built around 1910, the curved plant shelves are of reinforced concrete, like the lower walls of the structure itself. Capillary matting under a layer of gravel keeps the clay pots moist.

LEFT: Wide slatted shelving of white-painted hardwood matches the glazing bars.

BELOW LEFT: Tiered wooden shelves and a central plant stand are finished with a dark stain to complement the dining furniture.

RIGHT: This three-tiered wooden stand is an English design by Chatsworth Carpenters.

Brackets, Pots, and Decorative Details

Plastic pots have no place in any conservatory, whether modern or traditional. Apart from looking unattractive, they are impractical, inhibiting transpiration and drainage, and contributing to overheating of the plants. Simple clay pots, either partly or wholly embedded in compost or gravel, absorb and release moisture through their natural porosity and at the same time allow plants to remain the focus of attention.

Brackets, hooks, and plant supports should never take visual precedence over plants; simplicity is best. A rusting Victorian shelf or an eccentric terra-cotta planter almost always contributes more to the atmosphere of a conservatory than an elegantly coordinated range of modern designer ceramics.

LEFT AND RIGHT: Whimsical details in this late-nineteenth-century conservatory in Wiltshire, England, include shells and several fossils dug out of a collapsed grotto in the garden. A Victorian cast iron stove is now of decorative value only, and various pieces of pottery and statuary sit happily among the flowers and plants, which include cissus, begonia, gloxinia, mimosa, various geraniums, and an apricot oleander.

Shades and Blinds

Even with adequate ventilation, a conservatory can become an oven in the months of high summer without some added shading. Permanently installed blinds or curtains can be chosen from a wide range of styles and designs, from aluminum roller blinds to treated cotton and canvas. Most important is that the material remain unaffected by dampness, although some people prefer to create a living room effect with standard fabrics and simply put up with having to replace them regularly. Inexpensive alternatives to blinds and curtains include plastic film or temporary shading "paint" to cover the glass during the hotter months.

ABOVE: *Vaulted glass repeats the curve of a dramatic garden room, whose blue-and-white-striped roller blinds add yet more color to a very original scheme.*

ABOVE LEFT: *Light canvas ceiling blinds shade a narrow apartment balcony. It was converted into a conservatory/ dining room just wide enough to accommodate tables and chairs in durable teak.*

LEFT: *Country cotton lace dresses the lower panes of an artist's studio, leaving an uninterrupted view of the Parisian rooftop above.*

RIGHT: *The top story of this double-height conservatory in Languedoc, France, is the main bedroom. White lacquered rice straw blinds shield the room from the bright southern sun.*

LEFT: Narrow white louvered blinds shade an all-white conservatory looking onto a tiny plant-filled terrace. Only the view of the Eiffel Tower reveals that it is high above city streets rather than in the country.

BELOW LEFT: Rustic blinds of split bamboo produce interestingly striated patterns on the walls and floor.

RIGHT: People take precedence over plant watering in this conversion of a small Victorian conservatory in a London townhouse. Frilled cotton festoon blinds match the cushions and table linen (all by Laura Ashley). The hanging baskets are "planted" with candles at night.

BELOW RIGHT: Grapevines trained along wires just under the roof provide perfect dappled shade in summer, and their leaf fall allows more light when it's needed in winter.

Flooring

Although the conservatory itself may be furnished in an eccentric style, from Gothic to Raj, a more conventional approach needs to be taken with the choice of flooring. Wood, quick to swell in damp and heat, is almost always impractical. Instead, use tiles, slabs of stone, or brick. You can establish original patterns or arrangements by borrowing ideas from floors of buildings devoted to cool airiness, from churches to Mediterranean villas. The stunning patchwork floors of many late-nineteenth-century churches, in geometric, tessellated patterns (made by inlaying differently glazed clays), are now being reproduced by some flooring specialists.

Marble tiles are comparatively good value in view of the grand effect they produce and the coolness they provide. Travertine is easily obtainable and, though naturally pitted, can be supplied filled. Riven slate too looks impressive, but if you are defeated by its short supply and expense, consider concrete slabs, which, when wax polished, at least imitate the effect of dark slate.

For more rustic, cottagey conservatories, there is a wide choice of quarry tiles or the more biscuit-textured terra-cotta ones in different shapes and sizes, including octagons, hexagons, and the twelve-sided clover-leaf shape, which looks spectacular but requires hours of patient grouting.

If you plan to hose everything down to cool the room and the plants, your floor should be laid on a slight slope leading to a drain. If you are tempted to lace your whole floor with wrought iron grilles, as in Kew Gardens, you will have to insist that your female visitors wear flat shoes so they do not get heel-trapped in them.

ABOVE LEFT: *Gleaming dark slate contrasts with mossy bricks outside.*

LEFT: *Creamy tiles were inset with black diamonds for dramatic effect.*

RIGHT, *top left to right: Basket-weave brick, Victorian tiles, and terra-cotta tiles. Center, left to right: Mosaic, gravel, and brick paving. Below, left to right: Wood flooring, off-white ceramic tiles, and man-made "lawn."*

LEFT: *In a glazed room used more for living than for plants, coir or sisal matting is a practical and pleasantly natural floor covering.*

BELOW LEFT: *Unglazed tiles in two different colors make an interesting pattern, especially when combined with panels of iron grillwork.*

RIGHT: *Black and white tiles laid in a diamond pattern are formal and dramatic and create an optical illusion of width in a narrow lean-to.*

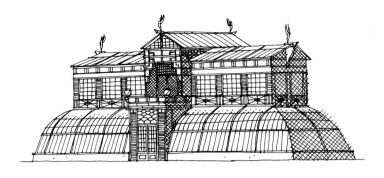

THE COOL CONSERVATORY

Many gardeners consider the cool conservatory to be the ideal one, as its modicum of artificial heat allows you to overwinter tender plants, to cultivate successfully some tropical plants, and to extend the flowering season of those pot plants which can be kept in a cold conservatory (even helping them produce winter blooms). A cool conservatory will provide for almost all the plants that grow in temperate zones, although what is temperate for a plant—a winter minimum of 40°F but maximum of 55°F, with good ventilation and partial shading in the summer—may be too chilly for human comfort.

But for those who are happier keeping conservatory heating costs down, and who are prepared to stay as cool as a lettuce (cucumbers, contrary to the saying, prefer it warm), the cool conservatory is far easier than a warm one to stock from local nurseries, and will generally be more colorful throughout the year.

The climbing vine *Cobaea scandens* is a very satisfying plant to begin with, as it can scale thirty feet of conservatory wall and roof in one season, if provided with taut wires for support. Unfortunately, though, its cup-and-saucer flowers, which turn from pale green to violet as they bloom, have, for some, an unpleasant scent, unlike the lovely, strong fragrance of *Jasminum polyanthum*'s pinkish-white flowers. This

LEFT: Morning glory (Ipomoea), nicotiana, geraniums, clematis, begonias, fuchsias, asparagus fern, and that Victorian favorite, an aspidistra, flourish in Cecil Beaton's conservatory.

plant is a vigorous climber, which—once it has reached the roof—will cascade down and form "layer roots," given good light and plenty of water in summer. *Passiflora caerulea* (passionflower) is a tough, fast-growing climber (growing even faster in a heated conservatory) with palmate leaves and complex bluish flowers. It needs to be cut back hard in the fall to keep it tidy, kept moist in winter, and well watered in summer.

Three particularly pretty "old" climbing roses are Nipheos, Maréchal Niel, and Rosa Banksiae Lutea—all with pale yellow double flowers, blooming in early spring. Narcissus will flower throughout spring if the bulbs are planted in rich loamy compost in autumn and then plunged into sand, ashes, or peat in a cool, dark place until leaves appear, when they should be moved to good light and, once flowering, into the warmth, in moist soil. Among the garden varieties to select for their smaller flowers are Cheerfulness, Thalia, and Rippling Waters. Specialist narcissus are even prettier, such as Paper-white; Soleil d'Or; *Narcissus bulbocodium* or hoop-petticoat narcissus, with small petals and large cup-shaped trumpets; *N. jonquilla*, about a foot tall, with tiny deep yellow flowers in clusters; and *N. juncifolius* and *N. triandrus*—both small varieties.

Streptocarpus × hybridus—the Cape primrose—has a long flowering season, from May until October, with foxglove-like white or violet flowers on long stems with wrinkled, velvety leaves. Keep it well watered and shaded in the summer. Watch for aphids and get rid of them as fast as they appear.

Pelargoniums divide into four main types. The "zonal" pelargoniums—or what most of us call geraniums—were popular with the Victorians for their winter blooms and distinctive brown "zoned" markings on the scallop-edged leaves. The Carefree hybrids, with their bright pink, white, or scarlet flowers, will bloom for a long time if kept at 45°F in the fall, in good light. Ventilate when it's warmer; this will also help to combat gray mold. Ivy-leaved pelargoniums, particularly the L'elegant variety with its variegated foliage, look attractive in hanging baskets, or—based in a ten-inch pot—grown up a conservatory wall. Royal pelargoniums are showy plants with frilly flowers in white, pink, crimson, and purple with darker veining, and pleated pink-edged leaves. Pot cuttings in loamy compost in spring or late summer, and keep just moist in winter. Water and ventilate well in hot weather.

Some pelargoniums have particularly aromatic leaves—used in Victorian times for infusing syllabubs with the scents of rose, pineapple, or orange. *Pelargonium crispum*—a bushy variety of up to two feet—will produce pink or pale violet flowers from spring to autumn, and lemon-scented fan-shaped leaves. Mint-scented *P. tomentosum* is a low-spreading climber which has white blooms throughout the summer. It will grow well above two feet if regularly repotted into larger size containers.

The tender varieties of fuchsias are best suited to the cool conservatory and can be trained in different ways—as standards, shaped bushes or pyramids, in borders or pots or hanging baskets.

Ordinary nurseries provide a small range of the varieties, while specialists offer the fuchsia lover a vast choice. To help prevent flower drop in summer, stand potted fuchsias on trays of moist pebbles, water well, and spray the foliage. In winter fuchsias should be cut back heavily and kept just moist. Root young shoots in sand in spring and be on the lookout for whitefly.

The basic primulas, such as *Primula malacoides*, *obconica* (leaves can cause skin irritation when handled), and *sinensis*, are all grown in vast numbers by big commercial nurseries; the plants are raised in perfect conditions and sold at just the right moment in all kinds of places, from nurseries to supermarkets. They are all actually perennials but are usually grown as annuals; it is possible to persuade your shop-bought plants to flower again but you will probably not get such perfect results a second time. *P. malacoides* is especially pretty: the flowers are borne in tiers and come in a range of beautiful pinks and mauves; they are powdered with little white flakes known as "meal" and are much admired by primula buffs. They can be grown from seed, which should be sown as soon as it is ripe; the seed container should be placed under a sheet of plastic or glass and kept in shade; a temperature of about 60°F is required for germination. A large group of primulas of assorted colors would look wonderful on a conservatory shelf or on a plant stand.

Another species which has a large fan club is *P. auricula*. They are not commonly available; you should look for specialists who cater to *auricula* fanciers. The specially hybridized varieties are extremely expensive; they have been developed over two hundred years to produce a large range of subtly bizarre colors—yellow, green, oxblood, dark brown, purple, violet, and indigo so dark as to be almost black. They all have white "eyes," some dark-ringed, and some are powdered with the much prized white "meal." They are as beautiful as the decoration on old Meissen or Chelsea plates; in short, they are living antiques. They like soil containing peat and leaf mold and plenty of coarse gravel.

Cyclamen, too, are universal favorites. Several garden forms of the species are available with their petals plain or ruffled, in white, pinks, and reds. They can be bought as pot plants almost anywhere and at very reasonable cost.

The more obscure cyclamen species can be bought as corms or, better still, grown from seed; in all cases, rarer species are smaller, more delicate, and more subtly colored than the garden varieties.

Ipomoea tricolor is the well-known morning glory and needs no description. It grows like a weed in hot climates, and is a marvelously decorative addition to conservatories in cold and cool temperate zones. Heavenly Blue is the commonest and most beautiful variety. It is an annual and seeds can be bought anywhere; it should be sown where you want it, either in groups or in wide pots with some tall, twiggy supports or canes, in a border, or on a trellis or wires.

Thunbergia alata, or black-eyed Susan, should be treated in the same way as ipomoea, but it is less vigorous. There is another climbing thunbergia—*grandiflora*, which grows into a much larger plant, with beautiful pale bluish-purple flowers.

Because there are so many varieties of camellia, it would take too long to list them here. All are handsome shrubs with lovely dark glossy leaves and single, double, or semidouble flowers in a vast range of shades: white, pinks, reds, and variegateds. A small number can be bought from ordinary nurseries, but if you want lots of variety you should go to a specialist who can offer you a wide choice.

Osmunda regalis is the royal fern, which commonly grows wild in Ireland. It looks very different from most ferns, as its fronds, which can reach three feet long or more, are bipinnate; the outer ones are sterile and the inner ones are erect and have sterile pinnae at the base and fertile pinnae covered with spore capsules forming a panicle at the top. In common with other large ferns, the fronds uncoil in a most fascinating and delightful way, to resemble a bishop's crozier. Osmunda likes a compost of turfy loam and peat, and shade. It is not pest-prone, but it can be very sensitive to powerful insecticides used on other plants.

Another very popular fern is the maidenhair of the Adiantum genus, A. capillus-veneris, although the whole genus is often referred to by this name. The adiantums must be the most quintessentially Victorian of all plants. George Nicholson's Illustrated Dictionary of Gardening of 1884 describes seventy-eight species. Several species of adiantum are available from good nurseries and fern specialists, e.g., A. hispidulum, tenerum, and venustum. All need a damp atmosphere and can be planted in commercial peat compost in pots or in the borders. They need subdued light and are ideal subjects for a north-facing conservatory; if your conservatory is a sunny one you can place them in pots or in a bed underneath slatted shelves, where they will grow beautifully in the subdued light. They can be propagated by division or by spores in spring; if you place pots of suitable compost near the plants you will soon be able to see the minute plants developing.

ABOVE RIGHT: Antirrhinum majus (snapdragon) lends dramatic color.

RIGHT: A flock of birds of paradise (Strelitzia reginae) fills one end of a small conservatory.

137

Vine planted outside the conservatory & trained through a hole in the wall, up between the staging & onto wires. Stretched between the roof rafters.

Roses —
Banksiae lutea
Maréchal Niel &
Niphetos,
climbing up wires.

Pelargonium —
Regal Zonal &
species in pots.
Vast choice.

Narcissus
varieties &
species.

Ferns under
staging.

Homemade
pots,
containing
Lilies &
fuchsia.

Lily species planted en masse
in large pot or tub. This works well,
provided the species chosen
flower at the same time.
Most of them need staking.

Morning Glory sown in pot
and trained up canes.

Narcissus in pot
on table.

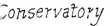

Conservatory

Fern in a hanging basket.

Passiflora caerulea is the only one that will stand a cool house. Similar habit to Jasmine, but deciduous. Very vigorous, the tendrils reach out groping for a victim.

Jasminum polyanthum.
It likes to climb to the full height of the conservatory and then cascade down. Evergreen. very vigorous.

Camellias in bed. They like coolness and shade Vast range of whites, pinks, and reds.

Raised bed faced with tiles.

Standard fuchsia numerous varieties.

Black-eyed Susan sown in pots and trained up canes.

Primulas in pots on stand.

Royal fern in bed, very sensitive to pesticides.

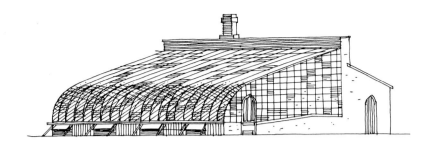

THE WARM CONSERVATORY

Since you are more likely to have planned a heated conservatory for your own comfort, rather than for that of your plants, you should establish only those plants which can endure a dry, centrally heated room in winter (with a cooler night temperature) and a surfeit of sunlight in summer. Most temperate plants, however, do best in a steady 65°F temperature by day throughout the year, combined with 50 percent humidity and little direct sun. Fortunately, there are ways of growing temperate plants without having to adapt yourself to a shaded, very damp, and tropically tepid conservatory.

Grouping plants together, for instance, allows them to share the humidity of their collective transpiration. If you have central heating pipes along a wall in your conservatory, hosing them down occasionally will produce temporary clouds of steam, which the plants will enjoy.

Thermostatically controlled heating will ensure plants are kept warm at night (at around 50°F) when your furnace is likely to be turned down in the rest of the house. And in every conservatory there are areas cooler than others, which will suit certain plants. Ferns, for example, prefer the longer hours of shade on the northern side. Plants needing lots of light, like variegated varieties, always thrive better in west-facing positions.

Apart from making it more comfortable for people, the

LEFT: *Among the warmth-loving plants in the conservatory of The Dairies, Castle Howard, Yorkshire, are arum lilies, orchids, and spiky exotic palms.*

extra trouble and expense of heating a conservatory makes it possible to grow a much wider range of plants. With a minimum night temperature of 60°–70°F you will be able to enjoy the heady scent of *Gardenia jasminoides*, the reward of picking your own oranges, lemons, or limes, and the lush tropical look of ferns and palms. Among the more spectacular palms is the large dark-leafed *Howea forsterana* (Paradise palm), the kind that used to be seen in fashionable tearooms of the 1930s with a palm court orchestra playing nearby. These palms should, therefore, be kept in shade, well supplied with water and soft symphonies. The *Dicksonia antarctica* tree fern can grow, slowly, to a magnificent six-foot spread of soft green, finely divided fronds, if given the space, shade, and a high level of humidity. (It will also grow in a cool conservatory.) Another tree fern, *Davallia*, is characterized by furry brown creeping stems called rhizomes, which can be shown to advantage in a hanging basket lined with sphagnum moss. *Cyperus papyrus* grows quickly and will be thrusting against the conservatory roof in only a few years. It is almost impossible to overwater it in summer; grow it in an undrained pot filled with richly manured soil.

In a well-heated, well-humidified conservatory, showy, fast-growing climbers from South America will flourish in the tropical atmosphere. The flowers of bougainvillea are small, but are clasped in vivid magenta or lilac-rose leaflike bracts. *Bougainvillea speciosa*, the best-known variety, is vigorous but thorny. All bougainvillea should be grown in terra-cotta pots or in a well-drained bed crocked with a layer of broken brick or pot. *Passiflora caerulea* is a rampaging climber with complex, exotic flowers in lavender and white. Their coronas of filaments are said to resemble Christ's crown of thorns, hence the common name passionflower. *P. quadrangularis* has dark crimson flowers with maroon and white striped filaments. It is the *P. edulis* that bears fruit. Just as bizarre and beautiful are the frilly scarlet and gold flowers of the *Gloriosa rothschildiana* and *superba*, curvaceous climbing lilies with curly tendrils. They need light support to climb on, and are easy to grow from seed

in high temperatures.

Two climbers which can also be grown in pots or borders are *Stephanotis floribunda*, the white bridal flower with a delicate jasmine scent, and *Mandevilla splendens*, with its bright, rose-pink large flowers and dark, glossy evergreen leaves. *M. suaveolens*, with heart-shaped leaves and long, fragrant white flowers, does not, however, do well in a pot and should be grown up a trellis. All like plenty of warmth and need generous watering in summer.

Shrubs are useful fillers. *Plumbago auriculata* is a decumbent (sprawling) shrub which is also a fast-growing climber. It has ice blue flowers and a great summer thirst, and will also grow happily in cool conservatories. *Nerium oleander* is tidier, a slow-growing evergreen with double or single white, pink, red, purple, or yellow flowers. (Leaves are highly toxic.) It can also be grown fairly successfully in a cool greenhouse. *Datura* (*Brugmansia*), the tropical relative of the English thorn apple, with its pendant, trumpet-shaped flowers and horned petals, will do well in a border if cut back in winter and fed in summer with liquid manure. (Turn solid manure into liquid by infusing a sack of it in a barrel of rainwater, like a giant teabag.) The *D. arborea* (again, the leaves are poisonous), *wrightii*, and *suaveolens* plants are very fragrant and very grand-looking. *D. sanguinea* bears scarlet and orange flowers. All are, unhappily, prone to attack from red spider mite.

There are several particularly exotic lilies worth looking for. *Zantedeschia aethiopica* (arum or calla lily) has a fleshy white "spathe" wrapped around a yellow spike; it needs good light and plenty of water until the flowers have faded. *Vallota speciosa* (Scarborough lily) holds bright scarlet, funnel-shaped flowers on very long stems and needs moderate watering but lots of warmth. Both can survive at the top end of the warmth scale in a cool greenhouse.

Also in the lily family are the *Agapanthus* species. With lots of watering they are easy to grow in a wide range of temperatures and are stunning to look at with their round heads of blue flowers on tall, stiff stems like drumsticks.

All tall, bulbous plants look even

better with a planting at their base of green saxifrage or sedum.

The real fun of a heated conservatory is in growing the small, cultivated varieties which will, if the temperature is as high as the Victorians kept their "stove houses," eventually bear fruit. Lemon trees are easy to grow from seeds; one of the hardiest varieties is Meyer, but it will not grow at all under 55°F. Kumquats (*Fortunella*) will fruit all year round if looked after carefully; it is particularly attractive, with its pretty bush shape and numerous tiny oval orange fruit. Other citrus species to consider are *C. aurantium* (Seville orange), *paradisi* (grapefruit), *reticulata* (mandarin, tangerine), *sinensis* (sweet orange), and *aurantifolia* (common lime).

Depending on space, other possible plantings in a warm conservatory can combine beauty with practicality. Sweet marjoram is worth growing for its fragrance alone, apart from its value as a culinary herb. Sage, thyme, mint, and parsley are also as attractive as they are useful. Eggplant, peppers, squash, and tomatoes are among the food plants that can be grown. Runner beans need plenty of space, but strawberries can be contained in a barrel or a decorative tower of pots.

RIGHT: A forest of tropical ferns below the delicate tracery of the dome in the Kibble Palace at the Botanic Gardens, Glasgow.

Musa acumirnta Dwarf Cavendish grows very tall and needs rich soil, plenty of water, and a very large pot or tub – like a half sherry cask.

Blinds on roof.

Mandevilla splendens.

Gloriosa rothschildiana, a climbing lily which needs support.

Coffea liberica

Unpainted hardwood staging supported on cast-iron pillars

Climber – Passion fruit growing on wire, stretched between pillars.

Many sorts of ferns can be grown underneath slatted staging, where there is limited light.

White Arum lily

Howea forsterana should be placed in a shaded position.

Conservatory

Cast-iron pillars with decorative pierced spandrels.

All plants should be watered with rainwater if possible. The downpipe from the conservatory gutters can be connected to a waterbutt or tank.

Papyrus grows very tall and should be planted in a very large pot or tub with rich soil kept filled with water.

Plumbago grows rapidly and untidily and should be trained on wires or a trellis.

Baby's tears can be planted in beds when there is little light to cover bare soil.

Half a sherry cask makes a good container.

Floor — small geometric tiles.

Dicksonia antarctica should be placed in a shaded position. Very sensitive to pesticides.

Delightful Profusions

Some conservatory owners plan their color schemes with control and decorator-style precision, favoring perhaps all-white flowers, all the shades of blue or pink, or a narrow combination of colors to fit the schemes of other rooms in their houses. Others, embracing the theory that there are no color clashes in nature, simply let their flowers run riot.

LEFT: Lavishly clustered flowering plants include magenta pelargoniums, multicolored schizanthus in a range of pinks and oranges, scarlet calceolaria, and lush begonias in hanging baskets.

CENTER LEFT: A bank of simple marguerites frame begonias, fuchsias, coleus, and ornamental Christmas pepper.

BELOW LEFT: Whites and pinks—cyclamen, tobacco plant (Nicotiana), ornamental allium, and primula—predominate, with a sunny touch of yellow cowslips.

RIGHT: Adaptable geraniums, in this case mature specimens of four to five years old, grow up a sunny wall.

The Pleasures of Potting

Cracked pots are smashed to provide a crocking layer for drainage in the new pot. This savagery is followed by the gentle art of tapping out the plant with its tangled root ball and placing it carefully on a layer of musty peat. More peat mixture is trickled around the edges and firmly tamped down, and the plant is then baptized in its new home with a soft spray of water. Few activities are better for the soul than a little potting in the shed.

LEFT: If conservatories offer celestial pleasures, the task of potting offers more earthly delights. In a cobwebby corner of a potting shed extension, bags and troughs of peat and toppling towers of old clay pots await the therapeutic ritual of repotting plants which have outgrown their original containers.

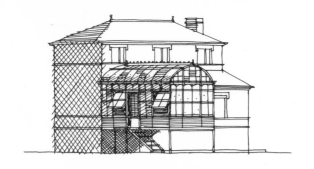

CHOOSING YOUR STYLE

Perhaps the most important consideration when planning your conservatory is its siting or orientation to the sun. The most rewarding conservatory is one that is bathed in sun for the greater part of the day so that for many months of the year free heat will warm not only the conservatory but adjacent rooms as well. You can take best advantage of this by careful air-movement management, which at its simplest means opening and closing connecting doors depending on the season and the time of day. More sophisticated methods involve fans, ducts, and double glazing, with supplementary heating and ventilation in extremely cold or hot weather.

Internal access and how you plan to use your conservatory are probably the next most important points to consider. No matter how glorious your sun-trap room, it won't be completely effective unless it relates well to the rest of the house. Conservatories are often used for dining and entertaining, so proximity to the kitchen and living room and easy access to and from them are key requirements. Guests will gravitate to the conservatory in any case, so a table for drinks and a small refrigerator in or near it will prove convenient on such occasions.

Although it comes last on the list of basic considerations, the architectural style of the main building should not be completely disregarded. A conservatory, however, is remark-

LEFT: Although it was added about three centuries later, this prefabricated conservatory is remarkably appropriate to the style of the late-seventeenth-century "Gothicized" manor house.

ably versatile. Since it does not block the flow of light or air to the inner rooms, it need not, with the exception of the lean-to type, necessarily relate in absolute terms to the house itself. Thus, it can usually stand in its own right as an individual expression of style, linked by whatever means is necessary to provide access. The more removed the conservatory from the constraints of its supporting building, the greater the stylistic freedom it can achieve.

An important consideration is the effect the building of a glasshouse will have on the garden or yard areas around it. Although it is a mainly transparent structure, it will nevertheless add another subdivision of space to its surroundings, perhaps even risking the creation of an unacceptably small garden. In this case the solution could be either a much smaller glasshouse or a much larger one enclosing the whole garden.

In judging the optimum size of a conservatory, the general rule is that one square foot of glazing can maintain four square feet of space at a temperature of about 66°–70°F, a calculation based on the difference between the amount of heat gained during the day and the amount lost at night. Opinions vary on the best material for framing the conservatory and usually aesthetic considerations hold sway. For retention of warmth alone, laminated wood has a higher thermal capacity than aluminum, though the latter is usually preferred where lightness and durability are important.

RIGHT: Many types of prefabricated glass extensions are available in kits, but because of the uneven slopes and odd angles of most older buildings it is advisable to have the construction overseen by a skilled tradesman.

Siting and Orientation

A simple rectangular house will permit an addition in a variety of positions, since in this respect it is the least restricting of house shapes. Choose the best sun orientation first, and then consider architectural treatments. Taking an absolutely purist approach to the precise orientation means aligning the central axis along a northeast/southwest line so that the extension is fully exposed to the southeast. However, since the conservatory's relationship to the garden is also very important, this axis can be shifted a little to accommodate and frame garden views.

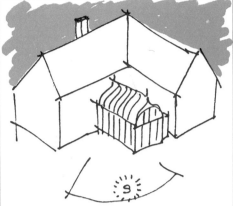

A corner site can be economical because you have to build only two new walls. In planning terms, more rooms can open into the conservatory and it can act as a linking space between rooms. The house also benefits more from the passive solar gain, as surface area contact is maximized. Provided the orientation is right, the solar gain in a sun-trap corner can be spectacular, and there may be less cooling because it is sheltered.

In this situation, with no appropriate simple wall to use as a "host," a more independent approach can be advantageous. Maximum exposure to the sun's rays and an individualistic architectural style can be achieved, possibly at the expense of wall area and less effective solar energy transfer to the main building.

Lean-to buildings are economical and good heat conservers if properly oriented, but they are usually less adaptable than some of the more self-supporting types of structures.

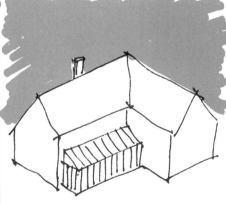

Lean-to structures, which depend on one or two house walls for support, inevitably mean less flexibility in siting decisions.

In situations where no suitable wall exists, a lean-to can be built against a new solid wall of its own.

Although it is the easy and obvious solution against a simple building, this conservatory will not receive much sunlight before noon.

A better solution, this conservatory is placed on the south side of the house, but it now faces the garden fence!

The best solution is to turn the extension around, directing the axis back into the garden. It could also be made longer than the house, protruding slightly in front to take advantage of northwest views.

Some buildings have such a strong character of their own that the style of the conservatory should be deliberately very different, as well as being sited apart from the main house.

When the conservatory is sited a little apart from the main house, a connecting corridor or access way helps different styles and periods complement one another.

Siting and architectural style have a strong interrelationship. A lean-to conservatory is often the most practical and aesthetically complementary shape for a long wall. Logically sited against the long wall of a stone house, this conservatory has been built with a stone plinth wall to link it in style to the main building.

Architecture

The addition of a glazed roof only will convert a room into a conservatory with minimum expense and effort. A greater feeling of height as well as an increase in light will result.

Conservatories can be used to link two buildings, with visual priority given to whichever is considered to be more important.

The requirements of orientation or space can dictate other choices of design for linking extensions.

Larger areas can be enclosed by a series of conservatory vaults.

Alternatively, both height and width can be increased to create large buildings, such as pool houses.

Appropriate landscaping helps embrace the conservatory's function as a bridge between house and garden.

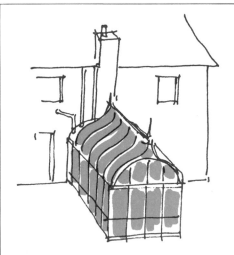

Pipes and chimneys can be accommodated with a linking unit; don't be put off by them, or try to avoid them at risk to other considerations such as correct orientation.

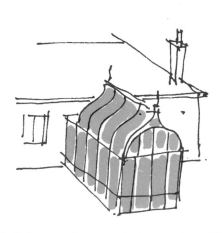

A link or valley can help resolve differences in level.

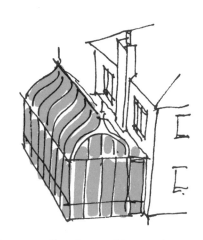

Here a valley is used to resolve problems of pipes, chimneys, and low upstairs windows.

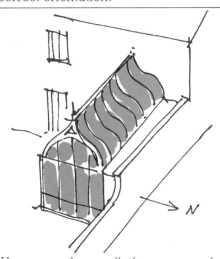

Use a garden wall if necessary for privacy. A solid wall on the north side is more effective than glass.

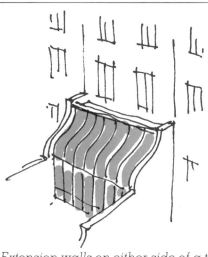

Extension walls on either side of a terraced townhouse conservatory can add privacy.

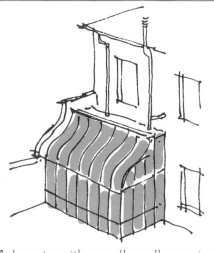

A lean-to with a valley allows pipes through it without modification of the curved glazing.

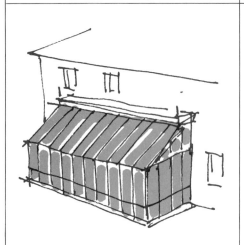

A simple lean-to conservatory is placed against an unbroken wall.

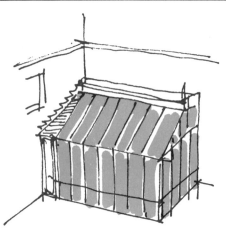

In a corner, if the walls are not at right angles, use packing fillets.

It is sometimes appropriate to build a long verandah in glass to link rooms.

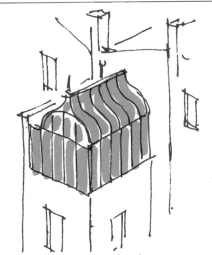

A conservatory may be the most practical way of squeezing in an extra floor in a townhouse.

Conservatories naturally enable a wide outlook. If there is a view to be enjoyed, take advantage of it.

A conservatory can often be fitted into an awkward corner. In this arrangement it might serve as a central living space linked to several rooms.

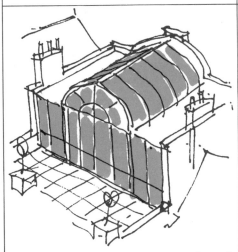

A rooftop conservatory can take advantage of otherwise useless space and may provide spectacular views.

It can be suitably integrated into the main structure so that it looks an integral part of it.

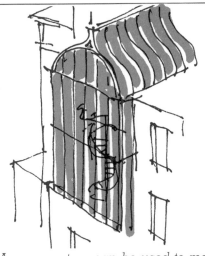

A conservatory can be used to make a dramatic vertical link between different rooms.

A penthouse conservatory is often easier and lighter to construct than a normal extension.

On a terrace the available space will dictate the size.

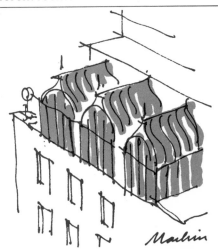

The shape can be varied to suit the architecture of the building and of its interior.

Building a Conservatory

As a general rule, the foundations of the conservatory should be dug to the same depth as those of the house. Most building codes require footings to be installed at a minimum damage depth below grade as a protection against frost damage. This foundation wall must be accurately dimensioned and true.

Drains: Roof leaders should be positioned at each end or at regular intermediate intervals. These leaders will drop into gulleys at ground level, and drains should be laid from the gulleys to an existing or new drainage basin, which must not be too close to the foundations.

Walls: Plinth walls can be built in masonry, and are particularly appropriate in conservatories with planting beds since damp earth against wooden walls would cause rotting.

Floors: Use materials that are not affected by water, such as tile, brick, or stone. Mats and carpets are only advisable if the conservatory is used primarily for a purpose other than growing plants, for example, as an office or dining room. A drain should be installed in the floor if possible to make cleaning easier. The substructure of the floor will depend on its planned use. Concrete is best for laying paving, although wood floors can be surfaced with a reinforced layer of concrete as a base for tiling.

The Superstructure

Conservatories may be bought as a kit or as a completed building. The apparent economies of using a kit may not be a reality in unskilled hands, as assembling unfamiliar components can take a great deal of time. In most circumstances, it is preferable to minimize the amount of work to be carried out on site, particularly glazing and painting, which are best done in advance rather than depending on weather conditions once the conservatory is in place.

Framework: Wood or aluminum are the most commonly used materials. Wood gives a warmer and more traditional feel, but is prone to movement and requires more main-tenance. Softwood, cedar, or hard-wood may be used. Cedar is softer than other woods, but has a high natural level of resin, which makes it less vulnerable to decay, but more difficult to paint. However, a variety of treatments are now available that protect all woods and finishes against rot and decay. Hardwoods should be used for sills and can be used else-where though they are more costly than softwoods. Aluminum frame-works, formed by extrusion, are usu-ally thinner than wood and incorporate sophisticated details to assist in assembly. Aluminum should have thermal breaks to prevent inter-nal condensation in cold weather and reduce heat loss. All fasteners should be corrosion resistant, partic-ularly in aluminum systems, where they should be of stainless steel to prevent electrolytic decay. Most well-designed conservatory systems use concealed fasteners. Glazed struc-tures rely on weatherproof seals between the glass and the frame-work. Modern aluminum glazing techniques use internal draining bars, which prevent leaks. Conven-tional systems using mastic or putty rely heavily on the assemblers' work-manship (and the right weather con-ditions) for the successful use of these sealants. They are more susceptible to failure due to settlement or thermal movement.

Glazing: Single glazing is a very poor insulator and in most climates the additional cost of double or triple glazing will be offset in a very short time by savings on supplementary heating. Special coatings on double glazing can further improve its insu-lation capability, and tinted glass can be used for solar control.

Flashing and junctions: Where a con-servatory joins an existing building, a flexible seal must be fitted. Lead, copper, or aluminum flashings are commonly used to form a mechanical seal (copper should not be used with aluminum). Avoid adhesive mastics and tapes, which rely only on the quality of the surface to which they are attached. Flat roofs and valleys should have an adequate slope for drainage, with appropriately formed joints in the covering material.

Paints and finishes: Conservatories are traditionally finished in white, which reflects light, but other colors, naturally finished wood, or alumi-num should be considered. Wood should be finished with a surface that allows it to breathe, as changing lev-els of humidity will inevitably cause moisture penetration. Avoid any sealants, varnishes, or paints that are impervious. Aluminum frames fin-ished with a baked enamel coating or anodized are very durable. Untreated aluminum will be quick to oxidize and in certain atmospheres will corrode rapidly.

Heating: Although a carefully sited conservatory will benefit from solar heating on most days, supplementary heating will usually be required, especially at night. There are various alternatives to consider: expanding the heating system of the house to cover the installation of electric base-board or unit heaters (easy to install, but comparatively expensive to run). Heat pumps: Heat can be brought into the conservatory from outside sources in various ways. Underfloor heating with either electric or hot water pipes is costly to install, but has the advantage of eliminating the need for visible pipes and radiators. This system is practical only with solid concrete floors. Ducted air heat-ing is useful if there is a pool in the conservatory. Grilles in the floor or at high level direct warm air over the glass surfaces. Heat can also be transmitted through hot water or steam radiators, sited around the perimeter walls.

Ventilation: Unless it is fully air-con-ditioned, the conservatory should be designed to permit cross-ventilation and an exhaust system for the hot air rising to the roof. This will cause a chimney effect, drawing in cooler fresh air from below. If the conserva-tory is to be used as a living room, stormproof ventilation will be neces-sary, since simple hinged ventilators let in the rain. Opening windows should be positioned to obtain maxi-mum cross-ventilation and easy access for cleaning the glass. Insect screens can be fitted if necessary.

RIGHT: An architect's sketchbook view of the ideal conservatory pro-vides a visual aide memoire to de-tails, methods, and materials.

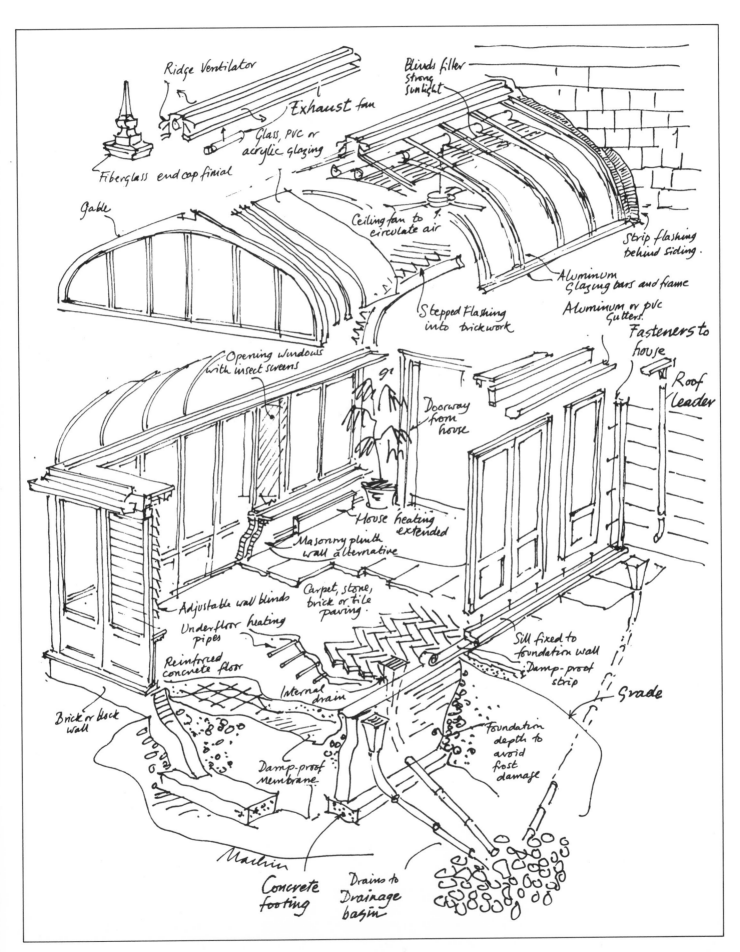

Ridge Ventilator

Exhaust fan

Glass, PVC or acrylic glazing

Fiberglass end cap finial

Gable

Blinds filter strong sunlight

Strip flashing behind siding.

Ceiling fan to circulate air

Aluminum Glazing bars and frame

Aluminum or PVC Gutters.

Stepped flashing into brickwork

Fasteners to house

Roof Leader

Opening windows with insect screens

Doorway from house

House heating extended

Masonry plinth wall alternative

Carpet, stone, brick or tile paving.

Adjustable wall blinds

Underfloor heating pipes

Reinforced concrete floor

Internal drain

Sill fixed to foundation wall

Damp-proof strip

Grade

Brick or block wall

Damp-proof Membrane

Foundation depth to avoid frost damage

Machin

Concrete footing

Drains to Drainage basin

RIGHT: *The painting* Lunch in the Conservatory *by Louise Abbema (1877) is reproduced by courtesy of Musée des Beaux Arts de Pau.*

DIRECTORY OF SOURCES

Greenhouses, Construction Materials, and Equipment

ANDERSEN
CORPORATION
ANDERSEN
WINDOWALLS
P. O. Box 12
Bayport, MN 55003
(612) 439-5150
*Low-maintenance,
energy-efficient windows
and doors for large glass
areas, incorporating
Andersen High-
Performance Insulating
Glass.*

BRISTOL FIBERLITE
INDUSTRIES
401 E. Goetz Ave.
P.O. Box 2515
Santa Ana, CA 92707
(714) 540-8950
(800) 854-8616; in
California (800) 422-2131
*Skylights available in
thirty-five standard sizes
and models. Also custom-
made in glass and
acrylic.*

DECK HOUSE, INC.
930 Main St.
Acton, MA 01720
(617) 259-9450
*Custom, contemporary
houses, including the
Conservatory Collection,
a series of passive-solar
designs.*

FOUR SEASONS
GREENHOUSES
425 Smith St.
Farmingdale, NY 11735
(516) 695-4400
*Passive-solar
greenhouses, atriums,
and solariums. A catalog
and the name of a local
representative available
on request.*

GARDEN WAY
SUNROOM/SOLAR
GREENHOUSE
430 Hudson River Rd.
Waterford, NY 12188
(518) 235-3332
(800) 343-1908
*Designed with laminated
wooden arches and a
complete system of solar
components.*

GREENHOUSE
SPECIALTIES CO.
9849 Kimker Lane
St. Louis, MO 63127-1599
(314) 843-4376
*Construction materials
and equipment, including
fiberglass, fans, shutters,
and heaters.*

JANCO GREENHOUSES &
GLASS STRUCTURES
J. A. NEARING CO., INC.
9390 Davis Ave.
Laurel, MD 20707-1993
(301) 498-5700
*A complete line of
greenhouses and solar
rooms as well as
equipment and
accessories such as
heating and cooling
systems, planting
benches, and watering
equipment. A catalog and
the name of a local
representative available
on request.*

LORD & BURNHAM
DIVISION OF BURNHAM
CORPORATION
P.O. Box 255
Irvington, NY 10533
*Greenhouses and
solariums as well as a
complete line of
greenhouse equipment
and accessories. For more
information and the name
of a local representative,
contact one of these
regional sales offices:*

LORD & BURNHAM
P.O. Box 255
Irvington, NY 10533
(914) 591-8800

LORD & BURNHAM
3475 Investment Blvd.
Suite 208
Hayward, CA 94545
(415) 782-6236

LORD & BURNHAM
Windy Hill
Executive Center
Suite 204
2470 Windy Hill Rd.
Marietta, GA 30067
(404) 980-1213

LORD & BURNHAM
7908 Route 14
Crystal Lake, IL 60014
(815) 459-3600

MARVIN WINDOWS
Warroad, MN 56763
(218) 386-1430
*Windows and doors in
over five thousand
standard sizes. Limitless
design capabilities for
custom-made windows.*

PELLA WINDOWS AND
DOORS
100 Main St.
Pella, IA 50219
(515) 628-1000
*Sunrooms and skylights.
Write for more
information and the name
of a local representative.*

SUN SYSTEM
GREENHOUSE CO.
60 Motor Pkwy.
Commack, NY 11725
(516) 543-7600
*Residential and
commercial greenhouse
installations throughout
the continental United
States. Superior
construction of elegant
energy-efficient designs.*

TEXAS GREENHOUSE
COMPANY
2771 St. Louis Ave.
Fort Worth, TX 76110
(817) 926-5444
*Prefabricated aluminum
or redwood greenhouses
designed for easy
assembly with step-by-
step instructions. Both
freestanding and lean-to
styles available. Staff
personnel will assist in
planning for specific
geographical areas. Free
catalog available on
request. Collect calls
accepted.*

TUB-MASTER
CORPORATION
SKY MASTER SKYLIGHTS
413 Virginia Dr.
Orlando, FL 32803
(305) 898-2881
*Skylights in square,
rectangular, or round
designs with single,
double, or triple domes.*

TURNER GREENHOUSES
P.O. Box 1260
Goldsboro, NC 27530
(919) 734-8345
*Prefabricated fiberglass
greenhouses in a number
of styles. Also a complete
line of greenhouse
equipment and
accessories.*

VENTARAMA SKYLIGHT
CORPORATION
140 Cantiague Rock Rd.
Hicksville, NY 11801
(516) 931-0202
*Ventilating or fixed
skylights in seven sizes.
Motorized units also
available.*

WASCO PRODUCTS, INC.
Pioneer Ave.,
P.O. Box 351
Sanford, ME 04073
(207) 324-8060

DIRECTORY OF SOURCES

*Premium-grade
residential roof windows
and skylights called
Skywindows®, with
Permatherm® construction
for energy efficiency.*

XENARCX, INC.
1063 15th St.
Sparks, NV 89431
(702) 359-4692
*Manufacturer of the XEN-
WALL Solar Gallery, a
greenhouse equipped
with motorized blinds for
control of solar collection
and storage.*

Plants and Gardening Tools

AQUA-PONICS, INC.
1241 E. Chestnut #M
Santa Ana, CA 92701
(714) 541-5169
or
1920 Estes Rd.
Los Angeles, CA 90041
(213) 254-1920
*Complete line of
hydroponic equipment
and supplies.*

CARTER & HOLMES, INC.
P.O. Box 668
1 Mendenhall Rd.
Newberry, SC 29108
(803) 276-0579
*Growers, hybridizers, and
exporters of fine orchids,
ferns, flowers, and
foliage. Retail sales
division on the premises.
Visitors welcome 8:00 A.M.
to 5:00 P.M. weekdays and
on Saturday mornings. An
Indoor Landscaping
Division located in
Piedmont, S.C.*

ENDANGERED SPECIES
P.O. Box 1830
Tustin, CA 92681-1830
(714) 544-3339
*Growers of bamboo,
palms, cycads, and exotic
foliage. Four issues of the
catalog and newsletter
available for $5.00.*

HENRIETTA'S NURSERY
1345 N. Brawley Ave.
Fresno, CA 93711-5830
(209) 275-2166
*Growers and shippers of
over a thousand varieties
of cacti and succulents,
including larger cactus
specimens such as
Christmas cactus and
rhipsalis. A yearly mail
order catalog is 25¢.*

ROD McLELLAN CO.
Acres of Orchids
1450 El Camino Real
S. San Francisco, CA
94080
(415) 871-5665
*Specializing in the
cultivation of all varieties
of orchids. Mail order
catalog available.*

**NECESSARY TRADING
COMPANY**
627 Main St.
New Castle, VA 24127
(703) 864-5103
*Catalog offers complete
selection of safe organic
pest controls, plant foods,
and soil amendments,
tools, and books.*

**ORCHIDS BY
HAUSERMANN, INC.**
2N 134 Addison Rd.
Villa Park, IL 60181
(312) 543-6885
*A 56-page full-color
catalog listing hundreds
of species and hybrid
orchid plants is available
for $1.00.*

SMITH & HAWKEN
25 Corte Madera
Mill Valley, CA 94941
(415) 383-4050
*A wide selection of useful,
durable gardening tools,
furniture, and
accessories. A full-color
catalog includes a wide
range of garden forks,
spades, pruners, and
trowels from England, as
well as a complete line of
teak furniture.*

Furnishings, Flooring, and Decorative Elements

**ARCHITECTURAL
FIBERGLASS**
1330 Bellevue St.,
P.O. Box 8100
Green Bay, WI 54308
(414) 468-8100
*A full line of indoor and
outdoor furnishings,
including seating, tables,
and planters.*

**BOMANITE
CORPORATION**
81 Encina Ave.
Palo Alto, CA 94301
(415) 321-0718
*Energy-efficient concrete
flooring made to resemble
wood, slate, tile, and
cobblestone through the
use of color, texture, and
pattern stamping.*

**CAL-GA-CRETE
INTERNATIONAL, INC.**
803 Miraflores
San Pedro, CA 90731
(213) 832-8381 and 832-8382
*High-density decorative
concrete flooring tile for
interior and exterior use.*

CERAMICA MIA
405 E. 51st St.
New York, NY 10022
(212) 759-2339
*Imported Italian tiles and
terra-cotta tiles.*

COUNTRY FLOORS
300 East 61st St.
New York, NY 10021
(212) 758-7414
*Importers and distributors
of hand-painted and
hand-molded ceramic
tiles and accessories.
Branches and
representatives in most
major cities of the United
States and Canada.*

COUNTRY FLOORS
8735 Melrose Ave.
Los Angeles, CA 90069
(213) 657-0510

**EMPIRE GARDEN
WEST, INC.**
225 Sunrise Hwy.
Lynbrook, NY 11563
(516) 599-7112
*Imported and domestic
planters and pots, and
wicker furniture, baskets,
and other containers.*

ERKINS STUDIOS, INC.
604 Thames St.
Newport, RI 02840
(401) 849-2660
*Imported garden
ornaments and containers
in English lead, Italian
carved stone, terra-cotta,
cast iron, and bronze as
well as a collection of
teak outdoor furniture. A
36-page catalog available
for $4.00.*

**THE FLORENTINE
CRAFTSMEN, INC.**
46-24 28th St.
Long Island City, NY 11101
(212) 532-3926
(718) 937-7632
*Ornamental garden
furnishings and
accessories, including
fountains, statuary, and
furniture.*

DIRECTORY OF SOURCES

FOSTER-KEVILL
15102 Weststate St.
Westminster, CA 92683
(714) 894-2013
*Traditional planter
boxes in a variety of
designs, including the
Classics series in wood
and the Estate series in
fiberglass with wood
detailing.*

INTERNATIONAL TERRA
COTTA
690 N. Robertson Blvd.
Los Angeles, CA 90069
(213) 657-3752
*Imported Italian
planters, statuary, and
fountains in terra-cotta,
hand-carved sandstone,
bronze, and marble.
Showrooms in Los
Angeles, Atlanta, and
Dallas.*

ADELE LEWIS, INC.
101 West 28th St.
New York, NY 10001
(212) 594-5075
*A wide selection of
containers for plants and
flowers in a variety of
materials, including
pottery, fiberglass, glass,
and basketry.*

LUZON IMPORTS
531 Albany St.
Boston, MA 02118
(617) 482-5012
*A complete selection of
baskets.*

MOULTRIE
MANUFACTURING
P.O. Drawer 1179
Moultrie, GA 31776-1179
(912) 985-1312
*Handcrafted solid cast
aluminum Old South
reproduction furniture
and decorative elements
in a variety of designs
and hand-rubbed
antique finishes.*

REED BROS.
6006 Gravenstein Hwy.
Cotati, CA 94928
(707) 795-6261
*Hand-carved, handmade
redwood furniture for
indoor/outdoor use,
hand-carved planters,
garden sculptures, and a
wide variety of garden
accessories.*

ROBINSON IRON
CORPORATION
Robinson Rd.
Alexander City, AL 35010
(205) 329-8486
*Cast iron vases,
fountains, statuary and
furniture based on
original nineteenth-
century patterns. Also
cast iron restoration and
custom casting.*

SCULPTURE DESIGN
IMPORTS, INC.
416 South Robertson
Blvd.
Los Angeles, CA 90048
(213) 858-8266
*Imported Italian terra-
cotta urns and planters,
limestone statues,
balustrading, gazebos,
fountains, and other
architectural elements.
Custom orders welcome.*

TERRA DESIGNS, INC.
4 John St.
Morristown, NJ 07960
(201) 539-2999
*Fine ceramic tiles made
to order in a variety of
designs.*

TILE DESIGNS, INC.
5001 Baum Blvd.
Pittsburgh, PA 15213
(412) 621-9991
*Distributors of ceramic
tile, marble, granite,
and brick.*

DAN WILSON CO.
Hwy. 401 North,
P.O. Box 566
Fuquay-Varina, NC
27526
(919) 522-4945
*Builders of fine garden
furniture in a variety of
designs. Catalog
available.*

ZONA
97 Greene St.
New York, NY 10012
(212) 925-6750
*English teak garden
benches, terra-cotta
pots, and weathered
estate furniture, as well
as gardening tools and
accessories such as
Japanese river rocks and
Mexican beach pebbles.*

General

GARDENER'S EDEN
P.O. Box 7307
San Francisco, CA
94120-7307
(415) 428-9292
*A mail order catalog
featuring everything for
the garden and gardener,
including plants, seeds,
tools, planting boxes,
benches, racks, étagères,
cachepots, and planters
in a variety of materials;
gloves, aprons, and
baskets; furniture and
decorative accessories.*

ACKNOWLEDGMENTS AND CREDITS

PHOTOGRAPHERS

Grateful acknowledgment is hereby given to the following for permission to use their photographs in the book.

Gert von Bassewitz, 102–3; Cecil Beaton/Sotheby's, London, 120–21, 134; Jürgen Becker, 44–45; Antoine Bootz, 49, 74–75, 76 top & center, 93 bottom right; Marina Botta, Architect, 114 top; Clive Boursnell, iv; Wulf Brackrock, 46–47, 55, 126 top right; Linda Burgess, 30 bottom, 31 bottom, 137, 146 bottom; Camera Press, 126 top left/Bassewitz, 43, 101 bottom right/Becker, 38, 108/Kurtz, 53 bottom/Rej, 84 bottom, 86, 131 bottom left/Schenkirz, 42 bottom/Schmutz, 78/Willig, 28 top, 106 bottom/Zeitz, 22, 70 bottom, 88 bottom, 101 top left & right; Gilles de Chabaneix, 50, 77, 89 center, 107 bottom, 110 top right, 114 bottom; Julian Charrington, 83, 101 bottom right; Stafford Cliff, 92 bottom, 115; Eric Crichton, 145; Devonshire Collections, Chatsworth, 10 right; Richard Dudley-Smith/Sunday Express Magazine, 62–63; Elizabeth Whiting Associates, 130 top/Gary Chowitz, 131 top left & bottom center/Clive Helm, 122 top & center/Michael Nicholson, 54 center/Julian Nieman, 90 top/Tim Street-Porter, 51, 128; ESTO Photographics, Inc./Peter Aaron, 104/Ezra Stoller, 53 top & center; John Glover, 26 bottom, 131 center right & bottom right; Nancy-Mary Goodall, 27 top, 29 center, 33; Pamela Harper, 95 bottom; Harry Smith Photographic Collection, 94 center, 146 top; Julia Hedgecoe, 20, 29 top, 67; Elizabeth Heyert, 91; Michael Holford, 27 center; Hunt Thompson Associates, Architects, 56 top; Pierre Hussenot, 30 top, 31 top, 36–37, 52, 54 top, 68 top, 82 bottom, 111 top, 126 bottom, 127, 128 top; Impact Photos/Pamela Toler, 10 center, 28 bottom, 132 bottom; The World of Interiors/James Mortimer, 59, 130 bottom/Christopher Simon Sykes, 66 bottom, 140; Ken Kirkwood, ii, 13 top, 24–25, 30 center, 32 top, 34–35, 58, 95 top, 98, 118, 133, 148, courtesy of Mr. Barton, Thornbury Hall Herb Garden; Jean-Michel Kolko, 68 bottom; Laura Ashley Ltd., 129 top; Library of the New York Botanical Garden, Bronx, N.Y., 11 right; Francis Machin/Machin Designs Ltd., 26 top, 54 top, 61, 82 top, 87, 150, 158; Maison de Marie Claire/Bailhache/Belmont, 89 top/Bouchet/Hourdin, 65 bottom/Chabaneix, 131 center, 132 top/Goudaut, 131 top right/Hussenot/Hourdin, 111 bottom/Korniloff/Bayle, 128 bottom/Pratt/Preis, 56 bottom, 57, 92 top/Rozes/Hirsch, 42 top; Norman McGrath ©, 65 top, 84 top & center, 105 top, 110 top left & bottom; Duncan McNeill, 32 bottom; Tania Midgley, 28 center, 147; David Montgomery from Real Life Guide to Kitchens © Condé Nast Publications Ltd., 64; National Portrait Gallery, London/Maull & Polyblank, 8 left; Bo Parker, courtesy of Shelton, Mindel Associates, 72; Cressida Pemberton-Pigott, 13 bottom, 26 center, 29 bottom, 146 center; Robert Perron, 48, 79, 88 top; Edward Piper, 85; Antoine Raffoul, 70 top; Patrick Roberts, 94 bottom; Laura Salvati, 96–97; Richard Schenkirz, 76 bottom, 107 top, 112–13; Fritz von der Schulenburg, 41, 60; Mia Stewart-Wilson, 10 left, 11 left, 12, 13 center, 27 bottom, 89 bottom, 90 bottom, 92 center, 93 except bottom right, 114 center, 125, 131 top center & middle left; E. Stoecklein, courtesy of Robert A. M. Stern Architects, 66 top, 80, 81; Christopher Simon Sykes, 124; Per Tarneberg, 105 bottom; John Vaughan, 69; Victoria and Albert Museum, London, Cundall & Downs 4/B. J. Turner, 11 center; Colin Westwood, courtesy of Benthall Potter Associates, 71; Andy Williams, vi

ILLUSTRATIONS

Grateful acknowledgment is hereby given to the following for their permission to use their illustrations in the book.

Bodleian Library, E. W. Godwin, Artistic Conservatories, shelfmark 19186.c.l., plates 3, 8, 9, 10, 14 & 16, 14–15; Ironbridge Gorge Museum Trust, 16; University Library Leiden, Collectie Bodel Nijnhuis, 1; National Portrait Gallery, London, 8 bottom, 9 left; Pau, Musée des Beaux Arts, 160; Trustees of the Royal Botanic Gardens, Kew, by permission of C. Dobson, S.A., C.B.E., 9 right; Royal Horticultural Society, Lindley Library, 7 bottom, 8 center, 18–19; Sotheby's, London, 5; Victoria and Albert Museum, London/Paul Furst, 3 top/R Hooghe, 3 bottom/Loudon, 7 top

The chapter heading illustrations are by Alan Austin.

OUR THANKS

To all those who so generously allowed their conservatories to be photographed and to the following people for their expert help and advice:

Alexander Bartholomew; Pamela Bullmore; Ann Cahn; Gilles de Chabaneix; Noel Channon; Sally Chappel (for photography at the Victoria and Albert Museum); Andrew Cliff, Clifton Nurseries; Eric Crichton (for photography at the Royal Horticultural Society); Dr. Brent Elliot (The Royal Horticultural Society); Sarah Elliot (Victorian Society); Tina Ellis; Michael Goulding; Joanne Greif; Shirley Hind (Architectural Press); Anthony Huxley; Ironbridge Museum Trust; Michael Jacobs; Alex Kroll; Lucy Kroll; Don Lavin, Architect AIA; Gilly Love; Candida Lycett-Green; Lothian Lynas; Bruno Manuel; Josephine Marston; Lee Mindel; Joceline Morrison; Teresa Nicholas; Nancy Novogrod; Christopher Owen; Andrew Petit; Simon Rose; Daniel Rozensztroch; Alison Rutherford; John Scott; Helen Senior; Lady Francis Seymour; Richard Simpson; Suzanne Slesin; James Sutherland; Susanne Tetsell; Megan Tresidder; Clive Wainwright (The Victoria and Albert Museum); Shirley Wohl.

The illustrations on pages 138–139 and 144–145 are by Julie Carpenter.

Special photography by Ken Kirkwood and Antoine Bootz.

Special thanks to our research associate Mia Stewart-Wilson, Francis Machin, our planning consultant, and Ian Hammond, for production artwork.

INDEX